Captivity Tales

Also by Elizabeth Hay

Crossing the Snow Line (1989)
The Only Snow in Havana (1992)

Captivity Tales

CANADIANS IN NEW YORK

Elizabeth Hay

Happy Birthday, Terri!

All good wishes

Elizabeth Hay

Dec. 1993

New Star Books
Vancouver
1993

The lines from John Wieners's "A Poem for Trapped Things" are
reprinted from *Selected Poems, 1958-1984* (Santa Barbara, Ca.: Black
Sparrow Press, 1986), by permission of Black Sparrow Press. The lines
from "SKETCH: A childhood place" are reprinted from *sunblue*
(Hantsport, N.S.: Lancelot Press, 1978), by permission of Margaret
Avison. The lines from "Stories of Snow" are reprinted from *The Book of
Canadian Poetry*, edited by A.J.M. Smith (Toronto: W.J. Gage, 1957), by
permission of P.K. Page.

Editor: Rolf Maurer
Cover illustrations: Barbara Klunder
Back cover image from *Outdoors Canada*, Reader's Digest, (c) 1977
Printed and bound in Canada by Best Gagné Book Manufacturers
1 2 3 4 5 97 96 95 94 93
First printing, October 1993

Publication of this book is made possible by grants from the Canada
Council, the Department of Communications Book Publishing Industry
Development Program, and the Cultural Services Branch, Province of
British Columbia.

New Star Books Ltd.
2504 York Avenue
Vancouver, B.C.
V6K 1E3

Canadian Cataloguing in Publication Data
Hay, Elizabeth, 1951-
    Captivity tales

    ISBN 0-921586-32-9
    I. Title.
PS8565.A875C3 1993   C818'.5407   C93-091899-1
PR9199.3.H39C3 1993

for Mark, Sochi, and Ben

Trapped Things

This morning with a blue flame burning
this thing wings its way in.
Wind shakes the edges of its yellow being.
Gasping for breath.
Living for the instant.
Climbing up the black border of the window.
Why do you want out.

JOHN WIENERS
A Poem for Trapped Things

Animal Life

This is June. The windows are open, screens in place, one onto the street, the other to the air shaft — that screen in contact with grey light, the soft material of trapped air. Light flicks the edges of grey brick, illuminates the dust, makes a line similar to mine as I move from one end of the apartment to the other. Soft out there, and so hard, so dismal, so much misery in that pearl grey.

Throat of pigeons, long throat of the air shaft, the dead of light.

They're gutting the buildings on either side of this one. Boards, pieces of glass, chunks of plaster crash down the air shaft and bounce off the walls. Every so often rubble bounces off our windows with a bang that makes my head snap around. This morning a workman hung his long white dink out the window and sent a huge stream of yellow piss in my direction. "This is for the lady," he said. "Yeah, lady, come and fuck my dick."

I backed into the shadows. Animal grey. Feminine grey. Pearl grey — fur.

My body scissors its way the length of the apartment, to the right around the desk, then a sharp left, then sharp right around the head of the bed, sharp right at its foot to avoid the crib. I walk the length of the living room avoiding chairs three feet apart. Left around the edge of the sofa, sharp right to get between the table and sink. Cutting the air, making a dress of it, soft, funeral grey, dress.

Each time I pass my daughter's bed she seems to be lying there in her light blue dressing gown — the hump of her back, and the bedclothes thrown to one side. It's the doll. I remind myself each time I pass — a doll.

ERRATA
This replaces the original page 3.

Animal Life

This is June. The windows are open, screens in place, one onto the street, the other to the air shaft,that screen in contact with grey light, the soft material of trapped air. Light flicks the edges of grey brick, illuminates the dust, makes a line similar to mine as I move from one end of the apartment to the other. Soft out there, and so hard, so dismal, so much misery in that pearl grey.

Throat of pigeons, long throat of the air shaft, the dead of light.

They're gutting the buildings on either side of this one. Boards, pieces of glass, chunks of plaster crash down the air shaft and bounce off the walls. Every so often rubble bounces off our windows with a bang that makes my head snap around. This morning a workman hung his long white dink out the window and sent a huge stream of yellow piss in my direction. "This is for the lady," he said. "Yeah, lady, come and fuck my dick."

I backed into the shadows. Animal grey. Feminine grey. Pearl grey — fur.

My body scissors its way the length of the apartment, to the right around the desk, then a sharp left, then sharp right around the head of the bed, sharp right at its foot to avoid the crib. I walk the length of the living room avoiding chairs three feet apart. Left around the edge of the sofa, sharp right to get between the table and sink. Cutting the air, making a dress of it, soft, funeral grey, dress.

Each time I pass my daughter's bed she seems to be lying there in her light blue dressing gown — the hump of her back, and the bedclothes thrown to one side. It's the doll. I remind myself each time I pass — a doll.

Our apartment is a railroad flat with windows at either end. A long spaghetti, Alec calls it. At night it's a long long walk to the bathroom.

I lean over the sink to splash water in my face and smell the smell again. I've already looked for a forgotten sock, a dropped diaper.

I hear the ruckus in the wall. Rats, I thought at first, but no — pigeon wings, the pigeons nesting on the sill outside, the window bricked in.

Alec identifies the smell. He comes into the kitchen and says, "Pigeons. Their smell is coming through the cracks in the wall." "No," I say, naive, smalltown, unfamiliar with pigeons and close quarters. But he's right. I put my nose to the wall and nod. The strength of the smell is determined by the direction of the wind.

I write home about it. The sad bad pigeon breath of New York. Bertrand Russell without the brain.

Last night voices drifted in from the stoop. Roxy and Lulu. Lulu's hair is short at the front and sides, but travels down her back like a tail. They were talking about rats.

Afterimage: hair on the water in the toilet bowl. I pulled it out of my brush and dropped it as a light brown clump into the bowl.

I wasn't present for the drowning, having relocated as my horoscope said I would — "remodel, revise, relocate" — I read the paper in a friend's apartment upstairs sitting on the sofa with the baby, a dark grey sofa.

The next morning, when I flushed the toilet, I thought of rose petals: the story I had read to my daughter the night before, the rat still at large, but the child thankfully sleepy, and a sound sleeper. Thumbelina — a girl the size of a thumb who slept in a walnut shell under a rose petal. The image of petals afloat in water, and a dead infant being bathed one last time. Rats eat babies, I thought over and over again as we tried to find it and kill it. Disposed of, afterwards, in the garbage can in the snow.

The landscape of the apartment changed. Every piece of furniture had a new meaning. The rat had hidden here, been cornered there, disappeared over there. Outside snow covered the rooftops like toilet paper.

We were sitting in the living room — I had a small manhattan, Alec was drinking hot cider — and we felt sure, he felt sure, that the rat though still alive was no longer in the apartment. He had scoured the rooms, he said, it can't be here anymore. The manhattan halfway to my mouth, I heard running feet. Feet, I thought, and the enormity of footsteps (rather than things knocked over or brushed against) sank in — with the sound itself.

"It could just be the noise of the building," he said and he got up slowly to look. But it wasn't. The broom thumped once, twice.

Alec waited. He sat up till one thirty in the morning, then fell asleep in his chair to be awakened by rustling in the kitchen. He went, pole in hand, and chased the rat from a shelf, missed, chased it from under the stove, missed; saw it disappear into the bathroom; closed the door. In the morning, when he opened the bathroom door, the rat was in the toilet. (There must have been poison behind the cabinet under the sink, poison makes them thirsty.)

At our victory breakfast the stewed prunes nauseated me, much as raisins in rice pudding nauseated me as a child — their distended bodies like the muskrats our dog brought home and left to swell up on the lawn.

First rinsing the bottom of the tub, I fill the bath for my daughter. A spider scurries up the side, and I hold myself. Then I put my finger down, let the spider crawl onto it, and deposit it on the floor. I pick stray hairs off the surface of the bath water.

Haiku House

We live in candlelight, the light of a skinned animal left on the forest floor. At Auschwitz the building that housed valuables taken off the dead was known as "Canada": animals and people stripped of their skins.

In the middle of the apartment a lamp is on. Here beside the window direct sunlight never enters, but at two in the afternoon the sun strikes the windows of the building across the street and for twenty minutes bounces into this room. While it lasts it is silvery, metallic, very beautiful. Moonlight, says Alec.

Our children look clean until we step outside into the light and I see sleepydust in our daughter's eyes, a streak of milk on the baby's upper lip, a bit of dried mucus in his nostril. Similarly, I'm surprised to see grey hairs in Alec's beard as we stand on the corner.

Living in semi-darkness, the accumulation of it, so many inches a year, so many feet.

Silence follows the loud click of the trap. We lift our heads and listen.

And now I hear more noises in the kitchen cupboard and brace myself for further possibilities.

Dark and tiny rooms, their darkness intensified by the bruises on my legs. Four corners — edges of desk, bed, crib, sofa; three on the east, one on the west — bash my left thigh and right knee whenever I veer off course. I walk from the kitchen down here to my desk and a copy of *The Narrow Road to the Deep North and Other Travel Sketches*. Basho. I picked it off a friend's shelf, captivated by the title. Is it good? I asked. Well, he answered, I'm not much for poetry.

I open the book to haiku and prose, Basho's journeys through Japan, and immediately get the idea to record my travels through the apartment in the same way. Linked prose and verse. Travelling the narrow road of the apartment to the deep north of my desk: the pictures of snow, caribou, musk-oxen, the uncarpeted subfloor, basement directly below; it's much cooler here. Then back the same narrow road to the south, to the grow light above a shelf of plants, the radio, stove, coffee. Air from the air shaft. Coolness without light. Temperature without movement.

> *old light still answers*
> *to its name, raises its muzzle.*
> *Dog bones. Drybones.*

> *haunted by the snowfall*
> *in a husky's over-pale eyes.*
> *New York. June.*

Basho came to the barrier-gate of Shirakawa, "the entrance to the northern region," and the ground, covered with thousands of white blossoms, resembled early snow. The "pure white blossoms of unohana, tiny and delicate."

In early June "the gentle wind breathes the faint aroma of snow."

The smell of going backwards. In Coppermine rooftops were covered with caribou antlers which were ground up later and sold as an aphrodisiac in China. It never got dark. We ate dried apricots and slept under the bones of love.

In Yellowknife I read without a lamp at midnight. Fresh coffee was on the stove and my dog at my feet. My friend David stayed up every night until two in the morning, so animated by the light that he couldn't sleep. He stayed up taking photographs and drawing.

Now the north is reduced to birchbark light around my desk, David's photographs of snow on the wall, and David, dead.

I pick petals off the page — a shedding peony — and read

about the sleep cycles of flowers, so tired, watching my daughter sleep, Sochi, for "flower."

In Inuit folklore children grew out of the ground as flowers do. Women out wandering found them sprawled in the grass and took them home and nursed them.

> *summer snow: children out*
> *of windows.*
> *four in the last twenty-four hours.*

In bed Sochi surrounds herself with all her possessions — red shoes, purse, two bags — as though her bed is an Inuit grave and she is taking a long voyage to the underworld.

> *snow underworld; honeycombed*
> *and the sound of snowfall,*
> *slide of honey*

> *no trees — antlers the only branches,*
> *their velvet shed summers ago.*

The apartment is a long piece of bamboo — light comes in at either end, but not much — a haiku house — one long seventeen-syllable line.

Summer

Basho carried with him a paper coat to keep him warm at night, a light cotton gown to wear after the bath, writing equipment, some gifts from his friends. He slept on a grass pillow (having written a poem about the door of his old home "buried in deep grass").

I put my head of hay on a feather pillow and smell cigarette smoke at three in the morning, then again at six. The window is open and we are ten feet from the street. Already it's the end of June, and I wonder where summer has come from. A stranger, it arrived without warning — no greenery, no breezes — a face without features.

I iron at the coolest time, before seven in the morning, and even so sweat runs down my face. I iron two dresses, the cotton cooler for its recent encounter with heat.

No clothing except this long room. Summer — this heat — dresses by undressing.

The northern meaning of dressed: to be gutted, cleaned, cut into haunches, roasts, steaks.

I imagine all the different kinds of New York snow. The kind that slides off a car roof into a still white street. The kind that defies gravity and sits higher on a clothesline than anyone would think possible. The kind that slides off rhododendron leaves when the sun comes out: leaf snow. The kind that doesn't ever fall. January non-snow. City non-snow. The kind we wait for — a woman dressed up and waiting patiently in a lawnchair for the snow that never comes. She goes back inside and, without a word, takes off her winter clothes and puts on lighter wear.

Under the shadow of an arctic wall hanging, I remember a flower whose scent, if breathed at night, produces erotic dreams. A pendulous soft-breasted flower with a smell of cloves; the dreams — of amorous journeys inspired by fur, impeded by snow, completed by morning.

An arctic wall hanging: hanging by one's neck from a snow wall. Here, we're strangled by heat.

Necklace of melting ice (ice cubes wrapped in a teatowel, the teatowel wrapped around my neck). Cooler memories.

While his boat lay crushed in ice, exuding the smell of wood and fear, Jens Munk scratched under snow for herbs. He crushed the leaves to extract their juices and cure his scurvy. Of sixty-four men only three survived.

Which is cooler, to read about people trapped in snow and

trying to get warm, or people trapped in heat and trying to get cool? I flip through Samuel Hearne's *Journeys*, into the second one now, where Matonabbee acts as his guide to the Arctic Ocean and ensures the expedition's success. "Several of the Indians were much frozen, but none of them more disagreeably than one of Matonabbee's wives, whose thighs and buttocks were in a manner incrusted with frost; and when thawed, several blisters arose, nearly as large as sheep's bladders."

The ceiling fan lifts the pages of the book: an illustration of Indian implements: canoe drawn from all angles, paddle and spear drawn with fine, precise lines, the page tattooed with the possibility of movement, the air restless, like sleep. On the opposite page is a description of a summer snowfall deeper than any seen at any time by even the oldest Indian. "The flakes of snow were so large as to pass all credibility . . . "

I pour out the basin of cold water in which I've been soaking my feet, return to sit at the table, and feel on the floor the cool spot the basin has left behind. Half an hour later, when I get up and walk away, I leave behind two invisible tracks of warmth.

In the morning a hot little paw touches my face — my daughter's feverish hand. I lower the blinds, and put her hands in a bowl of cold water. She lies under a white sheet and plays with a small white purse. It's quiet, except for the zip of the purse, the sound of her fingers. A snow underworld: warm, out of the wind, but cool. She whispers to herself, the blinds click (quiet, except for the creaking of tree roots in the soil).

Eight feet into the apartment, the light from the window falls off and lamps are needed to make your way. This gradation of light, contained in such a small area, luminous to the left and dusky to the right, turns this small corner into a piece of fruit in a leafy tree, one cheek clearly visible, the other nestled in semi-darkness. Apple of light, transparent fruit.

John Hornby carried this image in his mind when he went into the Thelon River country in the Northwest Territories — a wilderness of natural, nearly invisible plenty which flattened, emptied, as he starved to death in the winter of 1927. He and his two young companions had missed the caribou, spring didn't arrive till June.

He passed through New York in 1924. A friend reported in a letter that he went "for the purpose of delivering a fur coat to a Lady Friend who was then in South Carolina."

Two of the pictures above my desk were taken on the Thelon River near the spot where Hornby is buried. A photograph of a musk-ox, another of two running caribou. They hang beside David's photographs of Yellowknife and snow. AIDS gave David the look of a starvation victim. His movements were just as jerky as those described by Hornby's nephew who watched his uncle, his friend, and himself starve to death.

The stamp on David's last letter was a wapiti, an elk. His letters veered between frantic requests, unattainable plans, and a certain calm. Plans to travel to Mexico and France, to have exhibitions in major cities, to write a book. Requests to have me buy him carvings, prints, pelts, and moccasins.

And calm. The last letter began, "The sunlight has been trying to shine through a light cover . . . a few tiny flakes of snow are persistently drifting down. Winter. Seems like a long cold time. However, I am working on a series of winter photographs that I'm certain you'd like. Pruned topiary trees, three of them photographed against the snow."

Our door opens onto two other doors, each double-locked; a triple inclusion — inside, inside, inside. Out. Grey leaves grow up my legs and into my lap, a long summer skirt from my friend Rosemary.

We paint and put up drywall and in the process find long, brown, wiry hairs in the old plaster. Horsehair, a friend explains; it was used years ago to make plaster more solid. I keep a chunk of hair-wall on my desk.

> *I picked up the baby and*
> *fled from the rat*
> *to a long grey sofa.*

We say far north. Basho says deep north; Japan is such a small country, he walked everywhere. And that's the whole problem, that I want to go deep and instead I'm going far, glancing off things — while standing still. Seated in a railroad apartment with dirty windows. A stationary traveller. Never leaving home, and never getting home.

Fall

David died in September, and two weeks later the baby was born. David was bedridden the last month, comatose the last two days. He died at twelve forty on a Sunday morning. His mother was with him. His sister told me this on the phone. He didn't have the strength to focus his eyes.

In the hospital the baby's hands were tied inside long sleeves to protect his face from his own long nails. His hair was red. He had two red birthmarks on his forehead. They'll disappear, the doctor said, "except when he's angry."

I had a postcard of David Hockney's *Still Life with Apple* and focused on the apple during contractions; a card I bought for David but didn't send before he died. (Later, the baby's first word will be apple, and he will love to eat apples more than anything else.)

Barred light through windows, shadows on the bed, wind blowing through an empty womb. I check my watch before adjusting a diaper under the other breast to catch the drips, then lean back against the headboard: to be so alone, and yet the main accompaniment. A displaced child nursing a child displaced.

Strange and interrupted night life. The air is grainy and white as though the room is an old film.

I can't sleep. Then sleep, and dream I can't sleep.

When Sochi was born my own childhood came alive. Now Ben. And Sochi's infancy comes alive. She is three years old. I remember, am brought back to, those first few weeks — my distress as I nursed her in the middle of the night, so very nervous and lonely and afraid.

In the dark she calls, "I wake up." I go to her and in lifting off the covers feel the wetness again, and my irritation.

"Even through the diaper," I say. And then, "I can't be washing sheets all the time."

I pull her pyjama top over her head, pull her wet bottoms off, put on a T-shirt and her dressing gown, tell her to go and lie down beside her father. She does. From that position, lying down but not under the covers, she starts to cry, "I want mommy. I want mommy." Softly. Tears.

I sit on the edge of the bed and wish there were room enough for me under the covers but Alec, the baby, and my daughter occupy the full width. Cold and full of self-pity, I say, "Come here," and she climbs over Alec and I hold her for a few minutes.

With the first baby my mind was full of all the bad things others might do to it. With the second baby, all the bad things I might do. This summer I was reading about a small child whose father often found him hiding in a cupboard, humming to himself. Years later the father discovered that the mother, a very young woman, had jabbed the boy with pins when he was a baby. Now, as I pierce a diaper with pins, I remember the story. And another about a child covered with small burns, triangular, from the tip of a hot iron. The thoughts sicken me and won't go away. I imagine my hand driving the pin into the baby's skin, and his cry of pain, every time I change his diaper.

Surely it wasn't like this with the first child. In those days didn't all the dangers come from outside? I had imagined our car being struck by another car, the baby falling, a pillow in the wrong place, a small coin within reach . . .

Yesterday we spoke slowly as though it was late at night rather than mid-afternoon, the words slow to come and often wrong: we wouldn't wish them away, yet how changed our lives are. How hard not to be able to do what we want. "Do people just suspend their lives," my friend Theresa asked, "until their children are grown?" Appalled at the way her life has already been suspended. "Is it terrible to want something more?"

Her small face, short dark hair, hands cupped around a mug, sitting only because forced to. She had forgotten her keys and was waiting for Bill to come home and let her in. Under the conversation ran her counting: the minutes as they went by, the months without daycare, the years without a job. Her eyes, as we drank tea, stayed stirred up by her counting. Measuring her resentment (against Bill who had said he would be there in an hour and wasn't after two) in that tiny fluorescent kitchen, which isn't even fluorescent yet appears to be.

The absence of shadows is tiring. In the kitchen a lamp with a one hundred watt bulb is trained on the ceiling. The living room is too dark for shadows.

Only here it is different. This spot of papers spread out beside a window, and light spread as wide as the papers (no wider), of words sought to articulate the emptiness, and windows framed to receive window boxes, no window boxes there.

I write: She had entered a confused and tiring time. As soon as I write "entered" I feel better. I am somewhere, after all. Somewhere confused and tiring, but somewhere. I am inside something, and the notion calms me.

So Canadian? This desire to be inside?

Writing in 1884 about the Inuit of Baffin Island, Franz Boas compiled a list of customs. The mother gives birth alone; cuts the umbilical cord alone, either with a stone spear head or by tying it through with deer sinews; eats nothing for five days except meat killed by her husband or by a boy on his first hunting expedition; remains excluded from her own house until a few days after the birth. Loneliness — isolation — all in the context of that snowy light. The sensation, those nights soon after giving birth, that I contained nothing but weather.

Winter is coming. It reduces us to the apartment, and reduces the apartment even more. Windows, difficult to open, are closed. The leaves of the tree of heaven (scrawny city sumac) turn yellow. Some leaves have fallen. I switch off the kitchen light and walk to the front of the apartment, to this pale light, too pale for October, November light in October (we've missed another season).

The Inuit word for starvation means *in between*. In between summer and winter when it was hard to hunt — the snow too soft, ice too treacherous. In between lives — this period with a new life which isn't my own.

The First Remove

I see things more than my mind can grasp; and the only way to save oneself from madness is to suppose that we have all died suddenly before we knew, and that this is part of another life.

ANARULUNGUAQ
*Greenlandic Inuk, upon
seeing New York in 1924*

Strangers

He tried to come in through the door, young, slender, in blue. Having grabbed Theresa — the two of us pushing ·the door shut, she on her knees by this time, me too, having fallen somehow, the stroller in the way. And then her face reared back, "No, oh no, please don't."

"Take it," she said. And he grabbed her chain.

Her cigarettes, the smell of them now as I write. She was so rattled she smoked two. She had seen something I hadn't, and I had seen something she hadn't. I told her later. "I saw your face."

"Fear?" she asked.

"Yes, you were frightened."

But it was more than that. Not having seen the gun, I didn't understand. Only after he grabbed her chain and fled. Stay down, she said, he has a gun.

Her small pale face — pleading. And then up on her feet as soon as he left, taking her twins out of the double stroller, comforting them. At first not obviously shaken, but welcoming a cup of tea and the cigarettes.

And now I'm sitting in the kitchen rather than by the window, away from the street. Frank Sinatra sings in the building behind, or at the side — one of the ones under renovation. Twice now, they've broken into our building through one of the ones under renovation.

The day began with Mexico. A jar of lotion bought on our last trip there, not opened till now. Overpowering, the recollections of my winter there: muddy coffee in clay cups, papaya, bread; the steps in the sun; elusive Alec; dogged me. Every time I turn my head, the reek of those days comes back.

The baby who screamed the most, who couldn't be

quieted, I realize now, was the one closest to Theresa, the one who saw it all. The other baby didn't see the gun.

At night it all floods up as though the bed is full of fear, possibilities, future. I imagine him standing at the front door as I try to get in while keeping him out. I imagine him right behind me, as he was, but quicker, so that the door doesn't close between us. (Did I have my key out already? Is that how I got in more quickly than he might have expected?) Every movement on the mattress pushes up another picture: he's inside the apartment, my daughter is screaming — and blood, lots of blood.

Theresa and I met in Mexico. In the picture on the wall behind me, she is one of several friends at a going-away party. Her face is tanned, she is pregnant with her daughter, I am pregnant with mine.

"I'm so glad they weren't there," she said of the two girls. "The sort of experience that could change their whole lives, the sort of thing they'd never forget."

Whereas the twins are babies and will forget.

Impossible even to have a name for him, a label. *Man with the gun, Burglar, Robber.* None fits. None covers the unfolding sequence of hand gesturing to his mouth for something to eat, fingers rubbed together for the alternative — money. None the patient manner in which he bided his time in the vestibule, or his smile of recognition when I came out as Theresa asked him, "Now who is it who's bringing you food?" Then the shake of my head, just as I had shaken it initially, he on my heels and knocking on the door behind me. Then the sudden surge as he grabbed her and she pulled back and we both threw our weight against the vestibule door. And then the gun.

A few hours later, Theresa passed him on the street. But he looked older, she said, so maybe not.

For half an hour, light enters the middle room so that it's like a cup holding light, the cup in my hands — wide, white, remarkably light for a place so constantly dark.

The library has switched from summer to winter scent. The heat is on. Sweet, like muffins.

Boas writes about the clothing worn by Inuit infants: birdskin when newborn, fawn and hareskin at one month, hareskin at two months. Their bellies were wrapped in sealskin as long as any part of the umbilical cord remained.

Matching this intimacy of infant with animal was the mother's rigorous distance from certain flesh. She wasn't allowed to eat raw meat for a year, nor was she allowed to eat any animal shot through the heart. She kept near her a small skin bag into which she put a little of her food after each meal, having first put it up to her mouth. Depriving the mother ensured the life of the child: the reverse of pregnancy, and about the same duration. For nine months she expanded, for a year she was diminished.

Baby — Ben. We stare at each other, trying to see something familiar. Everyone says we look alike. That's as hard for me to see as it is for him. What did I read? "He has seen nothing."

He sleeps in the kitchen where the light is almost always on, and when turned off leaves a darkness unusual for daytime. I watch his eyelids.

The doctor said, "I would know this was your baby anywhere."

Anywhere? Anywhere is a big place.

• • •

I drop things. Or rather, I pick them up and other things drop. It's as though my act of picking up crowds the room. The floor especially is cluttered by my simple activities whose purpose more often than not is to straighten, order, or at least finish something — clothe the baby, dry him, diaper him. Why does this happen? This incoherence, this spatial incoherence.

I drop love. It falls through my fingers. I can see it down

there on the floor and its shape just irritates me. The memory of the love I used to feel, and now don't.

Or — again — I don't drop love. I pick up one love and another drops. I pick up my love for my son and my love for my daughter drops to the floor.

Objects throw themselves, if you like. Love does the same thing. It throws itself out of me.

The diaper pail contained bleach diluted with water. Dirty diapers were in the water, I wrung them out. Then I set the baby feet first in the sink so I could wash his bottom. At once he grabbed the container of toothbrushes and spilled them into the pail.

In my anger that I hadn't foreseen the accident (but I had), my disgust at our toothbrushes floating in shitty water, my fury at a life of cleaning off, picking up, contending, I started to scream, "Fucking, fucking, fucking." I picked up the pail and swung it around and threw it into the tub, splashing the walls, the floor, my legs.

Alec arrived and I continued to yell, "Fucking toothbrushes in that fucking pail," and he took the baby and said nothing. He turned on the tap in the sink and said quietly, to the sink, "You could have just washed them off." Our daughter stood in the doorway.

I went with her into the kitchen, sat down, set her in my lap. "You shouldn't do that," she said, shaking her head and making a face that was half grin, half grimace. "You shouldn't do that." And we started to laugh. And laughing, still grimacing, she said, "That scared me, that bucket in the tub. It was like a monster."

Afterwards Alec acted and talked as if nothing had happened. When I pushed him — *respond to me* — and he didn't, I attacked him for not. Then he said, "The problem is you're so full of yourself."

I see him in the distance: it could be him. Same blue cap, beard, red checked shirt. He is sitting on a bench drinking a can of beer. Smaller than Alec. Even from a distance I can see that, but otherwise it could be him. He could be waiting for me.

When I see him walk away with the child — she is walking, he is pushing the stroller — and the child similar in age to ours, it could so easily be him with our daughter and baby. The sight of him moves me more than Alec has done for some time. I feel closer to Alec as someone else, closer to the suggestion of him than to the actual person.

I forget about the incident until this morning when he shaves off his moustache and appears with an upper lip I have never seen before. I note the vulnerability of skin exposed for the first time in fifteen years, and my withdrawal in the face of it. I feel more connected to his small shadow in the park than to this bared soul in front of me.

We joke about his new Mennonite look (he still has his beard).

His upper lip is boyish and wide, his smile a full smile, and touching. More visibly hurt. You can read the mouth now as well as the eyes. And yet the more of him I see the less in touch I feel. I am more comfortable with my feelings of sadness at his loss (the retreating figure in the park) than my feelings of sadness at his presence. And so it is with Canada. Away from it I can't think of anything else. When I return I don't know what to think.

I lie beside Alec in bed and watch his upper lip. It is so wide, a full page I haven't read before. His smile now involves much more movement and expressiveness — he is suddenly a much more humorous man. As a boy his lips always turned bright red whenever he ate an apple.

I wait for him to shave off his beard. I look at photographs of him as a boy, curious to see whether I will feel closer to or more distant from the stranger he will be.

That night he said he had thought about it all day.

"What did you think?" I asked.

"What we should do about it," he said.

"What else did you think?"

After a pause he answered, "Things can't go on like this. You so unhappy. It's dangerous."

The window is open and the air is cool. I came out of the library this morning to grey skyscrapers extending to the horizon and rain falling so hard that it looked like a long grey truck. A real truck splashed me from head to foot, and the man behind shrieked "Motherfucker!" when it got him. We start with the marriage counsellor next week.

I've been wanting to leave my preoccupations behind, but they're all I have. And yet how can I pursue them without it all being more of the same?

And then it occurs to me to write about other Canadians in New York, and I feel comforted.

Company

Plucked eyebrows, pale New York face. From under her bangs she asks, "What is the point of your book?"

My words and gestures become elaborate, excessively friendly. I say too much. I've grown timid, I say. I spend too much time at home, have no job besides writing and looking after kids, haven't done any radio work for two years; the book is a way of forcing myself to get outside.

Rouge, rose-coloured glasses, intense eyes. Looking at hers, mine start to water.

"The polite, cautious, apologetic nature of Canadians," I explain. "What happens to it in New York?"

"Well, I'm not very polite," she says.

She has lived in New York for twelve years. On the phone she said lunch, and I thought club sandwich. Instead we go to a French restaurant and the cheapest thing on the blackboard is an omelette for eleven dollars; I have ten dollars with me. We sit down and I check my pocket to make sure I have a subway token to get home. I open the menu, scan it with worried eyes, find some sort of chopped meat for $7.25.

She is friendly and wary, a Canadian journalist who can't figure out what I want. I tell her that I don't know what form the book will take. I just don't know. She tells me the book should be a personal account of my life in New York rather than a chronicle about Canadians in New York.

"Who really cares about Canadians in New York?" she says.

"I know," I say.

"Who cares?" she says again. "I mean it's like that speck on the sidewalk."

In the subway a young woman curtsies as she speaks in Spanish with elaborately polite phrasing, pleading with us to forgive the disturbance. I don't mean to show any disrespect, she says several times. The formalities are all very countrified. And then she just stands there. My hands are full with an apple, an umbrella, and a copy of E.B. White's *This is New York*, and so I don't give her anything. But she stands there so long, simply stands, with tears which may or may not be produced for effect, that I dig around in my purse, moved by her simple standing, made guilty by her mute waiting.

Fifth Avenue is splashed by light and the cars are bruised flowers. I'm surrounded by hard concrete, light air, music on the corner.

Inside I ask the librarian if it's always so cold in here. "Yes," she says. "For the books and paintings. And now that it's cold outside, I feel like I never get warm."

Her long, slender, black fingers sign a special pass for me to enter the photographic section where they keep Michael Snow. "What's the temperature?" I ask.

"It's supposed to be sixty-eight," she answers, "but it feels like zero."

In each book I read a different date for his arrival in New York. 1962, 1963, 1964. This book says 1964. In 1972, he moved back to Toronto and became active again as a jazz musician.

I turn the page and here's the Walking Woman, a cardboard silhouette with cropped head, hands, and feet. Snow had the image printed as a newspaper ad in the *Village Voice*, made up into stickers, painted on a car door, made into posters which he left on New York hoardings "to suffer," as one critic said, "the ravages of weather and anybody's casual vandalism." He photographed it in all of its stages: torn poster on a brick wall, reflection of same poster in a puddle, man walking past that reflection.

It's a haunting Canadian image — tattered by weather, ignored by passersby, yet persistent in its presence, continually sighted in the manner of the Virgin Mary. Beyond the subway turnstile, the cardboard silhouette is more commanding, once spotted, than all the shifting, winter-clad figures going by.

In a book about famous encounters, Snow recounts his meeting with Marcel Duchamp in New York. He explains how much he had always admired Duchamp, how much he wanted to meet him. He went to his apartment on 11th Street near Fifth Avenue, taking as a gift some rubber-stamped Walking Woman stickers. In the apartment he looked around and silently began to criticize everything he saw. Duchamp talked graciously but displayed no curiosity about his visitor, and Snow's mood turned more and more sour. In his mind he put down Duchamp for being commercial, worldly, egotistical — everything he claimed not to be — until by the end of the visit he despised him. Only when he stepped outside did he begin to doubt himself, begin to think about the "elevator ride" of ego: the neurotic descent to a sub-basement of jealousy and negativity, and the gradual ride back up into genuine appreciation.

We had been waiting for an elevator going down. One arrived, going up. My daughter hopped in with a smile,

"Here's the elevator!" and the doors closed. Her sobs climbed all alone to the top of Alec's office building.

The friend who was with me said, "She'll have to come back down."

We waited. The elevator came down and it was empty. My friend went up floor by floor while I waited with the baby who was sleeping in the stroller. He found her on the ninth floor where a woman was trying to comfort her.

Snow created "lost works" — posters and stickers of the Walking Woman — which he left all over New York. "Then there would be a connection which might or might not be seen." He went out at midnight and left behind a Walking Woman trail. In bookstores he slipped Walking Woman bookmarks inside books he thought appropriate. In the gallery he most wanted to represent him, he put stickers under the benches. "I could always say to myself that I was in the Green Gallery."

From 1961 to 1966, all his work used the Walking Woman image. A playful, disarming, mock way of making art and leaving his mark. At a party at Peter Jennings's apartment, he left Walking Woman stickers on the curtains, in the bathtub, in the closet, in the books, and in the bed. Jennings was not amused.

Wandering, lost as usual and trying to find the 49th Parallel Gallery. I've been walking past black wrought-iron fences on a narrow Soho street, townhouses flush with the sidewalk. I continue past small shops, cafés, the smell of tea roses from a basement shop, and into Jean-Paul Riopelle: his paintings of leaves in gold leaf. The catalogue on the counter shows a handsome dark-haired man, 1952, and the present grizzled artist who has been through a lot.

A young woman called Abbey shows me into the small library, takes down books and catalogues for me — three on Michael Snow, one on Joyce Wieland. Even with a New York haircut and fluorescent green earrings, Abbey looks like a Winnipegger: no makeup, steady prairie gaze.

"Canada's in such a mess," she says. "I don't even want to think about it. And it's so petty. I mean nobody sees the big picture. It's always 'my province, my wealth.' Why can't they get on to more important things — sign something that says Quebec is a distinct society . . . but you certainly can't forget the French speakers outside Quebec, and you can't let Quebec have any more powers than the other provinces."

Setting out in three lines the terrible complexity of it and why there never will be agreement.

I ask if she has any plans to go back to Canada. None at the moment; none for a while, she says.

Overwarm. Alone. Abbey has left. It's lunchtime and I pull out my peanut butter and honey sandwich, and my apple. One of Michael Snow's ancestors "invented" the Snow apple. His great-uncle, Charles Hammett Snow, was the Dominion pomologist in Ottawa. I haven't seen Snow apples since I was a kid, and they weren't common then. The flesh of the apple was remarkably white and had delicate tracings of red.

Snow is slender and much-photographed. In his book, *Cover to Cover*, he appears in summer scenes with many leaves, and then drives away in a truck. Halfway through, the pictures turn upside down in the typical Canadian format of half French, half English, each upside down from the other. Snow was born to a French Canadian mother and an English Canadian father.

A critic says that in his films Snow demonstrates how you can "make 'useless' time (random life-time) valuable." Which means that for himself, at least, he has found an answer to one of life's greatest riddles: how to find life where it barely exists. He would be good company in our apartment.

I find a book with pictures of Snow in snow. With his sister and dog in Chicoutimi, Quebec, 1937, when he was eight years old. Beside those pictures is one of snow falling outside a window, other windows beyond. *Snow Storm, February 1967.* New York.

Here is Joyce Wieland in a fur coat and hat.

Here she is with Snow. They lean, arm in arm, against a car; the Walking Woman is glued to the car door.

No one mentions the possibility of Joyce Wieland as source for the full lines of the Walking Woman. It was everywhere in their New York apartment. One visitor felt like an interloper. "When I sat down at a table, the 'table' turned out to be a walking woman lying on her side. I picked up copies of *Time* and *Reader's Digest* and they just 'happened' to have Snow's walking woman on their front cover."

In his article, "A Lot of Near Mrs.," Snow writes, "To 'cut-out' means to (slang) leave. Girl watching. Passing out of the picture and yes we'll soon be passing out of the picture."

Cut out, walked away from. As was Wieland after twenty-five years of marriage.

• • •

"Did it ever occur to you," the marriage counsellor asks me, "that Alec's long and mysterious sickness in Mexico was psychological? That he was depressed?"

Depressed, she means, at the prospect of leaving Mexico and living with me.

The counsellor is about fifty. She wears lovely brown leather pumps. I tell her I like them but she doesn't pay much mind. She has pretty legs too. I look at her face, already tired of this although what she is saying right now is interesting.

She says, "And that this was very hurtful for you, hurtful and undermining?"

No, that has never occurred to me.

I know that seeing a counsellor is helpful but I hate every minute that I'm in her office. When I ask for advice she says she needs to know more history. She calls it information gathering. We tell her where we come from (she says she learned everything she knows about Toronto from Margaret

Atwood), what our families were like, where we met. We reconstruct our movements from Mexico to Salem to Brooklyn to Manhattan and I find the physical effort of explaining the past enormous. I want to say to her, Do you know how much work it is to talk to you? You should be paying me.

Finding out about Joyce Wieland, on the other hand, is a joy. Her catalogue has all the intimacy and gossip that Snow's lacks — rich stories about growing up, frankness about her adult life, more than passing mention of her marriage to Snow: "We made each other," he told her when they separated.

Reading about her, I feel as though I've fallen into her life, and into my own. She was born on June 30, 1931 in Toronto. Her father died when she was seven, her mother died when she was nine.

"Childhood memories surface in her work: blood on the sheets, chalk on the blackboard, the loss that is unexplainable, the blue-lined foolscap that she loved."

Everything is here. A whole life shaped by childhood and saturated by memory. She was here. And now I am here. And by being here I will learn about her. Nothing is more vivid than early memories, I decide. Not childhood as it happens, but childhood as it is remembered. The layer under the layer.

Wieland says the red ink-staining in her work is "a really old memory of my taking care of my mother, her haemorrhaging, and blood on the sheet. It occurs all through my work — that red impinging on some white." It incorporates the menstrual memories which followed, and the infertility: the inevitable monthly stain.

In New York she made paintings and films, showed the films but not the paintings: "I felt that I had nothing to add [to the painting scene here], nor did I want to become part of it." Her work became more political, feminist, patriotic. She began to make quilts — a connection with her mother and sister, with women in general — and on those soft, sensual, warm backgrounds made statements about her love for Canada. In one quilt called *O Canada*, the white letters are scarlet-backed and "as they spell out the first verse of the anthem, they cast rosy reflections of 'glowing hearts' on the white 'arctic' ground."

Her quilted cloth assemblage, *109 Views*, was inspired by a trip she made from Toronto to Vancouver, and haunted by an earlier "very strong memory of a map being pulled down on a roller . . . this fantastic Board of Education map, beautiful pinks and greens, words such as Keewatin, Hudson Bay, and a tiny point at the bottom, Toronto . . . the unimaginable vastness of this, which seemed even bigger as a child . . . the words 'Dominion of Canada' in a big arc going across . . . and the description of the richness of this expanse."

In my mind I change the map of New York from one of a city where I continually get lost to a place with Canadian landmarks, orienting me, shoring me up; invisible anchors, where other Canadians have stayed and suffered and been happy. A new sort of mapmaking — not David Thompson exploring the new world and seeing so well its future, the Indians dispossessed and probably forever, but rather a rolling back of the map to reveal a snow underworld: the galleries, lanes, avenues along which small inconspicuous Canadians travel.

The Second Remove

Man is nothing but a mythical animal. He becomes man — he acquires a human being's sexuality and heart and imagination — only by virtue of the murmur of stories and kaleidoscope of images that surround him in the cradle and accompany him all the way to the grave.

MICHEL TOURNIER
The Wind Spirit

Biography

The Cree considered dusk a deceptive time, a time of blurred edges, "a good time to focus on a memory." In this apartment it is dusk all day.

Early memories — soft ones. My finger dipping into the butter dish on my way through the dining room after my afternoon nap. Inching on my back to see under my grandmother's corset as she tied the stays — soft accordion pleats of old plump skin. Sliding on my stomach down a snowbank — white snow white sugar, brown snow brown sugar — almost under the edge of the plough.

A hundred years ago a man pushed a wheelbarrow full of hot sweet corn through the streets of New York. Later in the summer he brought hot gingerbread "and when new corn-meal came, then he brought new cornmeal puddings and cream." Mint girls sold mint from willow baskets hanging on their arms. Black women sold baked pears "carried around in a deep glazed earthenware dish, floating deli- ciously in a warm bath of home-made syrup." In the summer of 1902, "all the bathtubs being full, they played the hose on the victims of sunstroke as they were brought into the Bellevue Hospital yard." Hundreds of horses died in the streets.

Minik was here. Brought by Peary in 1897, he came with his father and four other Eskimos, nearly all of whom died the first winter. After the death of Minik's father, the staff at the Museum of Natural History staged a fake funeral in the garden "to appease the boy, and keep him from discovering that his father's body had been chopped up and the bones placed in the collection of the institution." Several years later Minik found out. "He became morbid and restless," said his adoptive father. "Often we would find him sitting crying, and sometimes he would not speak for days." At seventeen, he

was living in a boarding house on 44th Street, still pleading
with the museum to give him back his father's bones.

A letter arrives from a friend in Yellowknife. He writes it
after spending most of the night snow farming: ploughing
and smoothing cross-country trails for a ski race in the
morning. Eight centimetres of snow had fallen the day
before. He and his partner were the two snow farmers, his
partner coined the name.

Because he is exhausted he writes in a loose, disjointed —
younger — style, less staid than his Christmas epistles and
completely charming. Show your daughter some of those
photos from the Thelon River, he tells me, of animals and ice
and eating breakfast under an orange tarp. Remind her
constantly that there is more to the world than the claustrophobia of New York. Tell her stories about what you did up
here. Help her to picture how clear and cold Artillery Lake
is with thirty miles of ice on it in June. Describe that exquisite
flavour of oatmeal dolloped into your bowl, swimming in
reconstituted milk.

After twelve years in the United States, Minik went home
to Greenland. He was nineteen. He had been adopted at the
age of eight by a fond but unstable American family: the
mother died; the father was fired; he and Minik moved into
a small flat. Minik failed at school, worked in construction on
the Sixth Avenue subway, ran away to Canada. When he got
to Greenland, he had to start from scratch. He relearned the
language and learned how to hunt. He even got married, but
he never adjusted to life there. He created for himself an
ultra-American persona of gunman, fugitive, thief par
excellence — a Wanted Man whose picture was plastered
across every front page in America. But his self-created
legend failed to satisfy and after seven years he returned to
the United States. He found work in New Hampshire as a
lumberjack, and died two years later from Spanish flu.

• • •

Emily Carr sat on mail sacks as she made her way up the west coast of British Columbia. No rail around the deck, the edge of the boat level with the water, small dog in her lap. She was looking for totem poles — like those which now reside in dim twilight in the Museum of Natural History.

It was Lawren Harris who suggested she visit New York, tempted her with a book of photographs. She lay awake all night, and despite her hatred of "enormous cities cram-jam with humanity" she decided to come. By train.

She stayed at the Martha Washington Hotel in a room "half a story higher than Martha's lounge" because she was terrified of elevators. The clerk led the way to her room and turned on the light. "It was never more than twilight in that room, but I liked it in spite of its dimness . . . My window opened into a well and I was at the very bottom; about a thousand other windows, tier upon tier, opened into my well."

Her fear of elevators wasn't claustrophobia but the sudden rise and even more precipitous fall — the fear of a cable breaking.

She met Georgia O'Keeffe. The most famous Canadian woman painter met the most famous American woman painter (all of Carr's biographies mention it, and none of O'Keeffe's). It was a brief encounter at Alfred Stieglitz's gallery, An American Place. Carr homespun and stout, O'Keeffe slender and full of disdain. Carr had just begun her late blooming — this was 1930 — having met the Group of Seven only three years before. She found some of O'Keeffe's things beautiful, "but she herself does not seem happy when she speaks of her work." The painter/patron to whom she spoke answered with an impatience Carr welcomed. "Georgia O'Keeffe wants to be the greatest painter. Does the bird in the woods care if he is the best singer?"

O'Keeffe was the most self-assured of women, Emily Carr was not. She was shy, prudish, self-belittling, sentimental, bloody-minded — expert at that particularly Canadian form of self-defense: we aren't as good, and who would want to be? She spent most of her time describing the millionaires she didn't (want to) meet, the elevators she didn't (want to) take. She dwelled on her unworldliness.

I walk to the Roerich Museum two blocks from our apartment, past Straus Park, a little triangle in the middle of Broadway built in memory of Isidor and Ida Straus "who were lost at sea in the Titanic disaster. April 15, 1912." The words are carved into the back of a long stone bench and are hard to make out. Smell of urine, almost barnlike: homeless, poor, around me. "Lovely and pleasant were they in their lives and in their death they were not divided."

A young woman pushes aside lacy white curtains to water the flowerpots on her windowsill. This way — going towards the Hudson River — there's a slight rise on 107th Street, and for a few yards nothing appears on the horizon but the tops of trees. Chinese menus stick through wrought-iron grill-work, and metal garbage cans sit on the curb.

The Roerich Museum is number 319. Emily Carr met Arthur Lismer in this doorway and together they visited several galleries that she otherwise wouldn't have seen: Lismer asked the elevator operators to come down gently. They saw works by Duchamp, Picasso, Braque, Juan Gris, Kandinsky, Dove, and on one level she refused to be impressed. "Why is that carrot stuck through the eye?"

She was afraid of New York. Afraid it would make her sick the way other large cities had. She escaped after a week. A photograph taken that summer shows her sitting on a folding stool, about to set off on a sketching trip to Kapoor, north of Victoria. Sensible shoes, dark dress, dog in her lap, hat pulled low over her ears; a stout, dumpy — once beautiful — woman with "a little soft English voice," fifty-eight years old.

A New York friend wonders why painters never paint trees.

I tell her that Emily Carr painted trees. My friend hasn't heard of her, doesn't know of the progression from Indian villages, to totem poles, to trees, to sky — doesn't know of the life shaped by a desire to get outside yourself and "find a new self in a place you did not know existed."

• • •

Go out into the world. The counsellor's words, and mine. She wasn't ready for us to stop seeing her (four weeks we said, and six months later we were still beating our gums). But we were firm, finally firm. We thanked her and felt enormously free of ourselves after we left.

Go out into the world. The message at the heart of every myth.

Today the smell of water comes through the window. The breeze is just right — it carries the river two and a half blocks and brings it in over the basil. "As beautiful a land as one can hope to tread upon." Henry Hudson, 1609.

What is outside the door? First the stoop, painted red by Roxy the potter. And then the tree. The tree appeared last spring, one of six planted on the block, a splash of green so welcome it reminds me of the Israeli punishment for Palestinian rebellion: bulldozing not only houses in that hot inhospitable land, but trees. We pick garbage out of the hollow around its base: beer bottles, flying paper, plastic bags, candy wrappers.

A linden. One of the other trees on the block is a honey locust with soft feathery leaves. The rest are pears which have small white blossoms in the spring.

On either side of the stoop, and enclosed behind a high wrought-iron fence, are the garbage bins. They sit on sandy ground in which the rats burrow. Eddy the exterminator came the other day. He pointed out five rat holes: tunnels which lead to their burrows. One hole is at the foot of the garbage bin below this window, four more are in the sand in front of the building next door. We saw two rats as we talked.

Eddy is very concerned that we appreciate him. He stressed
how serious he is about his work, and how much he wants his
customers to be satisfied. He hoped the bill he wrote for thirty
dollars wasn't too much (it itemized in great detail everything
he had done). He used to have a monthly contract with us,
and then people got fed up because they had more roaches
after he left than when he arrived.

If you turn left and walk towards Broadway, you pass the
back of the post office — a brick wall with a big garage door
through which the mail vans come and go. Mailmen come
and go too, pushing carts equipped with blue pouches.
Yesterday I overheard one mention a body found in Riverside
Park at 104th Street. "Somebody dumped a body there," he
was saying. Shot once in the head. A man walking his dog
found it.

At the corner of Broadway there's a carpet store, a lingerie
store, and Claude's Coiffure, haircuts $10. Across the street,
a café and a jazz club. At night the street is beautiful: blue
and green neon in the window of the nightclub, pink and
blue neon in the window of Claude's Coiffure, streetlights
which cast surprisingly little light, and fruit vendors who work
all night.

At night the darkness is natural, the life in the streets
natural too, but uncommon. Rather than the negative daytime harmony between the absence of light inside and the
blocking of it by the buildings outside, there exists a positive
harmony between the darkness of illuminated streets and the
darkness of an illuminated apartment. The bustle — sense of
life — an intimacy.

Roxy shapes clay on her wheel. Her shop is across the hall
from our apartment. Knees spread wide, she bends over the
wet clay and shapes it up, then down, then up again. A small
mirror, placed so that she can see the back of the clay, makes
this sexual procedure more so. Her pregnant belly is speckled
with grey and white clay which, when wet, is a dark red-brown.

Long black hairs — threads — curl out of her chin. Her hands are small.

This summer I was working at my desk, the window open, when I heard the arresting words, "I miss you already," spoken with such longing that I looked up to see a woman's arm outstretched. The rest of Roxy moved into view and, from the opposite direction, a man.

Roxy lives beside us and Lulu lives above. Lulu has always been hot-tempered and hot-tongued. After her parents were murdered in a land dispute in Mexico, she was raised by nuns. "I jumped out the window," she told me, "and there was nothing those nuns could do." Her sister, on the other hand, took it, and now lives with a man who beats her and once set fire to their baby.

Lulu jokes about kidnapping Ben. She takes him upstairs to her own apartment, saying as she goes, "I'm going to kidnap you." She never brings him back. We have to fetch him.

She says she wants to meet the man who made Roxy pregnant. Then says no, she wouldn't want to have a baby on her own.

Three years ago she was pregnant. She was still living with Ronny then, and he was thrilled. One day, when he wasn't home, she got into one of her furniture rearranging fits: she lifted the sofa, armchairs, table, television, bed. Two days later, she miscarried.

To want something so badly and then almost deliberately give it up. I do the same thing. I gave up Canada the way I gave up my dog, and then they become the source of all my stories.

• • •

It's cool and wet, and I bring the little tape recorder down here to my desk and put on Teresa Stratas. When I was growing up, my mother listened to the Saturday afternoon broadcasts from the Metropolitan Opera while I sat hunched in a corner of the chesterfield, reading. The chesterfield was soft — patterned, a faded green. And *chesterfield* not *sofa*. I tried to warm an arm, a thigh, in its curves.

Listening now, and the same feeling of something stirred up, wildly theatrical and out of place. New York in Wiarton. New York in Mitchell. New York in Guelph. The music came on loud, a torrent of emotion flooding a cold house. "When did you start to listen?" I asked her once. "Oh," she said, "in Renfrew when I was fifteen."

Her escape into opera interrupted my escape into a book and always reminded me of where I was. I associate opera with being cold.

Steam rises off the fountain at Lincoln Center, and small white lights glow in the trees. Across the street a young man makes cappuccinos in a small café. He is slender, rather short, olive-skinned; his open-necked shirt reveals lovely chest hair. He steams the milk in a metal container, pours it into a tall slender white cup, adds the espresso, then the cinnamon.

I sit at the counter and watch him. His shirt has light and dark grey stripes on a white background. He makes two other cappuccinos while I drink mine. To my right, rich chocolate cakes are displayed in a glass case. I pull out a scrap of paper from my pocket and jot down: memory of two Black Forest cakes baking in the kitchen in Yellowknife — midnight, one in the morning, two — the layers come out of the oven. My birthday. I was twenty-five.

Olive-skinned cappuccino maker. Warm profession. The man beside me moves his copy of Handel's *Messiah* so that I have more room, then takes huge bites from a very thick ham sandwich. When he asks his much younger companion if she feels better now that she has eaten, she says, "Thank you, yes."

I cross the street and enter the opera house. *Aida* is my mother's favourite opera and so I feel condoned, approved, and in her company. The "Great Golden Curtain" rises on the first act and I hear Milton Cross's voice on the radio, and my mother in the kitchen . . .

Now, in a reverse of childhood, I spend the afternoon with the opera close by and my mother at a distance. Between acts, I listen to the quiz my mother entered several times. She mailed her question and listened with veiled excitement to see if it was chosen. Edward Downs was quizmaster then. All those cultivated accents deciding if a question from Mitchell, Ontario was worth their while. It never was.

Teresa Stratas sings Kurt Weill, and I'm disappointed. Her voice seems forced. I crack open walnuts, inspired by her suppers of nuts and a banana, her lunches of half a pear.

Herbert von Karajan conducted her in *The Marriage of Figaro* and said, "If you want to sing Mozart properly, listen to Stratas." I look for a recording of *Figaro* by Stratas, can't find one and buy Jessye Norman instead. I put it on, listen for a while, put Stratas back on, and now she sounds good. She has a tough, unpretty New York sound, a theatrical, bleak and finally beautiful voice. I listen to the tape many times over the next few weeks, and in this apartment it seems the perfect thing to listen to.

Even as a child she had an enormous voice, what she calls a dark, deep voice: "In my parents' restaurant everybody was shocked at this skinny five-year-old who spoke like an old man." She sang everywhere. She sang at all the Greek functions in that part of Toronto, and in people's homes: "I remember being absolutely terrified. All that loomed in my mind was, Ah, someone might ask me to sing." She sang to her cat, and to the sewer rats in the basement. At night her mother cried so often over the unpaid bills that Teresa, still a child, slit her wrists.

She was sixteen when she heard her first opera. A customer who was drunk and couldn't find his wallet paid for his meal with two tickets to the Metropolitan Opera, on tour in Toronto. Teresa went with her brother. They saw *La Traviata*, and "it changed my life."

She lives not far from here in an old building in the Upper West Side. Reports say that her apartment is large with marionettes hanging from indoor plants, and colourful pillows on the sofa. Inside she wears loose robes in vivid colours, outside she could pass for someone without means: no makeup, drab coat, newsboy cap. She is a tiny, tempestuous woman — five feet tall, ninety-five pounds — with the same reputation for cancelling that Glenn Gould had. "So what?" she tells the *New York Times*. "I regret nothing."

In 1981, at the age of forty-three and at the peak of her career, she disappeared for almost eight years. For part of the time, she made use of the anonymity that New York more than any other city offers and hid out here. Those eight years coincided with the illness and death of her father, a violent manic-depressive who terrorized her as a child and whom she cared for in the last years of his life.

She calls her disappearance, which was in part a wounded retreat after her unhappy filming of *La Traviata*, "the most important journey of my life — to death and back, around the world and back. I did it right there on that sofa where you're sitting."

No wonder she lives here. Nothing is more un-Canadian than self-dramatizing hyperbole, no matter how truthful.

Moody, thoughtful, uninhibited, introverted. A hermit/ performer. Glenn Gould was the same: rapid-fire clowning and run-on brilliance set against solitude. His radio documentary, *The Idea of North*, was, he said, "a very dour essay on the effects of isolation upon mankind," and as close to an autobiography as he was likely to get.

Precipitation

Often the baby stretches his hand towards the window facing north. When I take him over there, holding him so that he can see out, he smiles and croons to the window and me.

In the winter, wet flakes as big as cigarette papers fell on the corner of 105th and Broadway. We stood under umbrellas, and I thought of David Thompson's comment that melting snow is wetter than rain; it penetrates a tent in a way that rain never does.

Beautiful — precipitation that is more than rain and less than snow.

"Light is falling," I say to my daughter. I look out the window as she sits up in bed. She peers out too — at the slice of pale light that touches the grey brick wall five feet beyond her window. Light falls like rain — an outside condition that never enters. We measure the inches.

Snow Seen is on the bedside table. It's full of sentences I don't understand, but the cover is white, and I like the title.

The book is a doctoral student's thesis about Michael Snow, and it makes for the sort of weariness you feel after an hour of looking in a museum.

When Marshall McLuhan lived in New York, he was invited to a conference at the Museum of the City of New York and irritated everyone by being interested in only one thing: why museums make us tired. He blamed our fatigue on the clash created by western "visual" culture imposing its sense of space on earlier "acoustic" cultures.

Why is it tiring to look through glass, and fascinating to look through a window? Because artifacts don't move, and behind windows people do? Then why is it tiring to watch one of Snow's films, and fascinating to look at his stationary walking women?

Full climates exist inside. In the Museum of Natural History, a glass case contains Ellesmere Island.

In the barrens we sat quietly and waited for animals to appear. A bird came by my head, familiar as a dog. Under low willows were piles of small droppings — blonde pellets — where ptarmigan had weathered a long storm. The air held the warmth: 11 p.m.

Talk shared across the light, or not shared. Just light. The ice had melted.

Meeting places between snow and fur. Starving musk-oxen lie down to rest and their long hair freezes to the ground; too weak to pull free, they die in that position. A baby slips out of his mother's hood at night and freezes to the floor of the igloo. A fox manages to work itself out of a trap only to freeze fast to a stone, held there by the moist action of its warm breath.

Through reading and writing I develop a loose web of connections, as rewarding as a friendship with a dog: companionable, no talk. It eases my homesickness, my sense of disloyalty about living here.

• • •

John Drainie, in the hot summer of 1955, came to New York with a limp and a taste for alcohol, to share a cramped flat and seek his American fortune. For years, he had been Canada's best radio actor. Lonely, mortified, miserably homesick, he called home every night and left after six weeks.

William Ronald moved to New York in 1955. Over twenty American museums bought his paintings as did every important collector in the United States. In 1963, he took out American citizenship and bought a house in New Jersey. Three months later, his New York gallery dropped him; two years later, he stopped painting. He moved back to Toronto, took up media work, and only gradually returned to painting.

In the summer of 1990, Jean-Paul Riopelle's exhibition in New York went unreviewed and not a single work was sold.

After six years as a film maker in New York, Joyce Wieland was left out of the Anthology of Film Archives in 1969. She was attacked by a psychopath the same year and returned to Canada in 1972.

Maurice

Last night I dreamt that Claude Lévi-Strauss showed me Rio. Although he was married, he was very attentive, especially his hands which not only stroked my head but my face in some sort of shamanistic way, revealing things to me, pulling the curtains from my eyes. I woke with several images of this sort.

A few blocks away hedges are in flower along the Hudson River boardwalk. It extends several blocks with the river on one side and family barbeques on the other: Spanish and the smell of water. In a few months the raspberries will be ripe — they grow among the rocks down by the water.

Last night we walked past two old men drinking on a bench, their bottle inside a paper bag. "Now look," one of them was saying in Spanish, "this business of fishing," as the other came out from behind a hedge where he'd been urinating. Both of them smiled and clucked at the children.

The paper has news of Canada, finally: three pages on Sunday after the failure of the Meech Lake Accord and the likelihood of separation. The articles stress that any changes will occur slowly: when Bourassa spoke on television, he flanked himself with both *fleur de lis* and maple leaf. The paper has a picture of the St. Jean Baptiste parade in Montreal and refers to the new flowering of the independence movement. It will happen, over time. Everyone believes that now. Ben's Canadian citizenship card has arrived; the crest consists of a crown at the top, the union jack and the *fleur de lis* side by side, and the maple leaf at the bottom. The text is in English and French . . . all the rights and privileges, all the duties and responsibilities . . . I look at it fondly, hoping it will still be good in twenty years.

I take out the tape of my interview with Maurice and listen to it. His light French accent is restful. It's midday. Our flowers in the window box are beginning to spread out and so is the basil.

When I first saw Maurice, he was passing the doorway of the office I was in. His colleague — the friend I was visiting — called out his name, and he stopped: tall, slender, rivetting purple tie, casual green sweater and pants. His slender fingers kept touching his upper lip, exploring the dryness — incipient cold sore?

He responded to my friend, and to me when she asked if he could help me, with an unforced graciousness which is very rare. Later I thought to myself, "Too good for this world," the phrase written beside the names of small children who die. He reminded me of David.

We sat on a sofa and he opened up his address book and gave me name after name of Canadians in New York. "You don't mind the word?" I asked him. He shook his head, smiled. "Down here," he said, "you get used to describing yourself as French Canadian rather than Québecois, and, after all, I have a Canadian passport."

He lives in a tall building on Park Avenue. On a Wednesday morning he opens the door for me, and this time he is dressed in jeans and his hair is loose. We lean my microphone against the sugar bowl and sit across from each other at a long narrow table in a studio apartment, windows to our right, a view of a church and apartment buildings just beyond. Two vases of orange tulips sit at either end of the table. On the wall hangs a photograph of a nude man, and on the fridge and in the bathroom postcards and photographs of other men — nude and available for love, or leaning against a bed, newly satisfied.

"What were you like in Quebec?" I ask him.

"In Quebec I drank too much. I was in my early twenties and thinking — if I stay here I will go to an office every day for the rest of my life."

He was twenty-three when he first saw New York. He and some friends left Quebec City in the evening, on a bus making the traditional Easter tour to New York. They crossed from New Jersey through the Lincoln Tunnel, over the yellow line that divides the two states, and into Manhattan. They stayed at a hotel on 47th Street just off Times Square.

"It was immediate love for this city," he is saying, "first of all for letting me be completely anonymous, no one you knew could see you, no one could sneak over your shoulder."

"In Quebec City everyone knows everyone. You're always the son-of, the cousin-of, the brother-of, something-of. And then there's nothing to do. Culturally — it's better now — there was one theatre group, no foreign movies, no museum at all; art galleries were completely uninteresting. It was a society of very conservative people, pretending they knew everything and very proud of their ignorance."

"Close your eyes," I say to him, "and think of Quebec. What colour comes to mind?"

"Beige."

"And if you think of New York?"

"Red."

He reaches for a book about Vermeer and opens it to a reproduction of a woman asleep at a table. The painting is in the Metropolitan Museum, and half a dozen times a year he goes to see it. "It's so easy to build a story around it," he says. "It's the end of the afternoon, she's been working in the house all day — you know how you feel at four in the afternoon — and she sits down at the table and falls asleep. She's probably expecting someone — the door has been left open — and everything in the painting says she's dreaming. There's a bench close to it," he says, "and I sit there."

I look through the book at other paintings by Vermeer, several of them portraits of women with letters: writing letters, receiving them, giving them to a servant to deliver. I see myself sitting across from Maurice, his enthusiasm dulled a little by an hour of talking about himself, reawakened by the painting, the change of subject. Midday. Both of us tired. Our cups of café au lait sit between us, nearly empty; the plate of purple grapes, lightened by an hour of nibbling, is off to one side.

• • •

Waiting for the train after saying goodbye, a kiss on each cheek, I open the book Maurice lent me and my thoughts are pulled into focus by one line. "He went through the lobby hoping for mail. His box was empty."

With green felt-pen, Maurice has circled the page numbers 17, 18, 19 — the pages about sleepwalking as a boy. The book makes me think in one direction of Maurice, and in another direction of my own childhood: "the sprinkle bottle she used to wet my father's shirts."

My mother sprinkled shirts, teatowels, serviettes, then rolled them up so the dampness would penetrate. The shirts were wind-hardened and bone-dry, then dampened and reshaped, then dampened further and softened more when we wore them.

My grandmother's fingers went through the wringer. She hit the safety catch with the other hand and rolled her hand back out. Those were the hands I knew: one of them flattened, with rings which slid around the fingers.

I remember multi-coloured chunks of glass imbedded in stucco, the gay and lethal decoration of a small house on Main Street. The girl who lived there, the father who was away a lot (a fisherman? on the boats?), and the teenage boy who chased his mother around the kitchen table with a carving knife.

Was it with her, the girl of the broken glass house, that I went into the post office and picked through the wastebaskets, already full of love for old mail? We walked home with our arms full.

On the other side of the wall mail arrives. Not the soft slip of letters on wood, but the crash of metal as ten mail boxes drop open at once.

The stamp is soft as silk. My mother erases the cancellation lines and reuses stamps. Her letters arrive, the Queen's face softened and feathery, sent and returned, sent and returned.

Canadian light in New York: soft, erased, in the upper right hand corner.

• • •

Here she is. *A Girl Asleep.* And here's the bench where Maurice sits.

Her earrings, the glint of something on her headpiece, of buttons in the leather chair. It's much larger than most Vermeers, and the light seems later than Maurice said. Not late afternoon but evening; she has been waiting longer.

The man she is waiting for isn't going to come. The text beside the picture says that radiographs reveal a man framed in the doorway, then painted out. The light is too low for late afternoon, the wall above her head is dark.

Maurice must sit at the end of the bench — like this — when he looks at it.

Is it the coolness of this room, added to the light, which makes me think it's much later in the day? Next to me a boy, a student, copies a Rembrandt self-portrait: easel, oils, plastic spread on the floor, bags of Utrecht art supplies.

Why do I see a sadder picture than Maurice? Is it because

I'm thinking of the woman he lived with for seven years, then painfully but amicably left for a man?

Fur Stories

In Riverside Park trees slope down to the river and the opposite shore is visible — glassy New Jersey, bleached, Miami-like. Early every morning two Asian women sit on a bench in the park. The younger, prettier one teaches the other English. This morning they were laughing.

Lofty shade trees line Riverside Drive. The trees are elms and likely to die, the man who designed this stretch of green went crazy. Frederick Law Olmsted had two nervous breakdowns and spent the last five years of his life in a mental asylum. He roamed the grounds of the asylum dressed in heavy coat and hat — a Glenn Gould figure: genius wrapped up in an ineffectual attempt to protect itself.

Glenn Gould was the son and grandson of furriers. His grandfather's business card read: Thomas G. Gould, Fur Salon, Designers and Manufacturers of Quality Fur Garments. From a background of fur came his obsession with warmth, his genius for touch. When he was just a few days old, he reached up into the air and wiggled his fingers as though playing piano. When he was old enough to be held on his grandmother's knee, he would never pound the keyboard with his whole hand. "Instead," said his father, "he would always insist on pressing down a single key and holding it down until the resulting sound had died away. The fading vibration entirely fascinated him."

In June of 1955, at the age of twenty-two, he arrived at the Columbia studio at 207 East 30th Street to record *The Goldberg Variations*. In a little room off to one side, he poured scalding water from a kettle into a basin and soaked his hands for twenty minutes (the length of time this room is soaked in light). "This relaxes me," he said. He sat down at the piano and rested his stocking feet on a small oriental rug.

In a small booth in the basement of the Donnell Library, I watch him. A black and white film made in 1960. The recording engineer treats him with the casual contempt practical people have for artists and with the friendly contempt Americans have for Canadians. In a joking but dominating way, the engineer talks about Gould as a hayseed who came to Columbia with feathers in his hair. "Now just a doggone minute," says Gould.

Gould is young, his shirttail hangs out, he plays Bach's *Italian Concerto* with a bandaid on the second finger of his left hand. The recording engineer is bald and unimpressed. "In the four years since I've known Glenn he's changed from a small town hick . . . "

"Now just a doggone minute, I've travelled in every Canadian province — "

"That's what I mean. You came to us with chicken feathers and straw behind your ears."

They roar with laughter. Then they talk about why Gould would never live in New York. He associates music with great fields of snow. As a boy coming back from the cottage on Sundays, he listened to the New York Philharmonic broadcasts and saw that landscape roll by.

His speech has the same contours, the monotonous tone and delicate construction of snow. This most fluid of Canadians wrote down everything before he said it, both questions and answers. "As is my habit," wrote Gould in 1977, "the 'dialogue' was entirely scripted by me — I have, in fact, not spoken a spontaneous word via the airwaves for at least a decade."

His American biographer describes his voice as "odd, nervous, clipped, self-conscious." Canada at its most fluid and eloquent is still, somehow, self-conscious.

Gould boasted about making 131 edits in a speech of two

minutes and forty-three seconds in his documentary on Richard Strauss — about one edit per second. He made his recordings very slowly, laying down two and a half to three minutes of music for every recording hour. As slowly as Cézanne, whose still lifes rotted before he got them painted.

In 1955, Leonard Bernstein and his wife Felicia got through the final month of her pregnancy during a summer heatwave by listening to Gould's *Goldberg Variations*. Cool Gould. In hat and coat, he carries his folding chair down the street to Steinway's to try out pianos. All the people he passes are in shirt sleeves.

The film maker asks if he can take some still shots of Gould at the piano. Gould — "Do I have to?" "What about a shot of your gloves on the piano?" "No. No! I've had quite enough of that kind of thing! No!" When the film maker comes to his cottage on Lake Simcoe, Gould sits in coat and scarf against a backdrop of children swimming. The film maker shoots his gloved hands almost surreptitiously.

In June 1965, Gould went north. He took the train to Churchill on Hudson Bay, a trip of one thousand miles, one day and two nights each way. On the ride up he shared a breakfast table with an old surveyor who opened their conversation by saying that Thoreau and Kafka had also been surveyors. The two men talked non-stop for eight hours: they had mid-morning tea, then lunch, then afternoon tea, and didn't rise from the table until four o'clock.

Gould taped interviews with the surveyor and four other northerners, drove up to Lake Superior, rented a motel room in Wawa, and spent two weeks sorting and assembling the radio documentary he called *The Idea of North*. It opened with these words, spoken by a nurse: "I was fascinated by the country as such. I flew north from Churchill to Coral Harbour on Southampton Island at the end of September. Snow had begun to fall, and the country was partially covered by it. Some of the lakes were frozen around the edges, but towards the center of the lakes you could still see the clear, clear water."

Gould's radio documentaries were music in another form. He played voices simultaneously as though they were duets and trios, and called the result "contrapuntal radio." One critic described *The Idea of North* as a stream of ideas and a pattern of sounds created out of five voices: "a sound composition about the loneliness, the idealism and the letdowns of those who go North."

• • •

Ernest Thompson Seton was six years old when he touched a freshly killed deer. "I remember how soft she felt as I put my arms around her furry neck and between her hind legs to discover that she was fashioned there like a small cow." When he was six and a half he saw a freshly killed woodchuck. "I can smell that peculiar musky smell, recall the flexible animalism of its lithe body, and see the three little whitecapped glands that were thrust out of its anus. Its fur is better pictured in my mind than any since; and with me yet is the mixed sense of attraction and disgust it conjured up."

I read about him in the light of a small blue lamp in the New York Public Library. His life has the feel of a tall and wonderful tale. A cross-eyed boy, small for his age and burdened by an abusive tight-fisted father, he escaped when he could into the glens and ravines on the outskirts of Toronto. When he was fourteen, he built a small cabin in one of the ravines and spent every Saturday there. "I gathered shells, feathers, curios in the woods, and arranged them on little shelves . . . stuck feathers in my hair, and cultivated an Indian accent. 'White man heap no good,' was a favourite phrase."

As a young man he travelled to London to study art, and lived in a cold room on a diet of bread, beans, and porridge. He slept on hard boards and "bathed my parts in cold water several times a day." "Perhaps his physical condition," says one biographer, "had something to do with the mysterious voices he began hearing in the summer of 1881."

At first he heard "weird ecstatic mumblings; then after a month or more, these mumblings took intelligible form. I heard my name, and strange words." The voice was gentle and insistent. It said, "A year from now you will be living on the Plains of Western Canada. You will there regain your health . . . Your future will be, not in Canada or London, but in New York . . . "

He called this mysterious Voice his "Buffalo Wind." He did what it said he would do. He spent two years homesteading in Manitoba where he studied nature, drew animals, made notes, and regained his health. Then he moved to New York City, arriving on November 23rd, 1883 with less than three dollars in his pocket.

Seton had his Buffalo Wind, I have my Pigeon Breath. This morning I was wakened early by violent knocks against the kitchen window. I looked down the length of the apartment from our bed to the kitchen and saw the movement, the soft white flashing, of pigeon wings. Assuming the noise had been that — much harder than usual but still the quill-like rapping of their wings on glass — I went back to sleep.

After breakfast I was washing the dishes, and the pigeon — it must have been the same one — reared up and thrashed at the window with talons and wings. In each talon, held the way a jewel is held by a ring, was a rock. The bird beat against the glass with enough force to break the window — or so I feared — and then flew up to a higher sill and found its balance on balled feet. The rocks must have been tumours that the bird was trying to shake off. What else could they have been?

Seton found a room on lower Lexington Avenue, and spent the next four days looking for an old school-friend for whom he had no address. In Central Park he was picked up by a man who bought him dinner, and then invited him to go to New Jersey to meet some friends. In their hotel room in Newark, Seton "found out what he was," spent a "mean and restless night" keeping the man at bay, rose early and left. In Manhattan he tried to sell his fur cap in a furrier's shop on Elm Street just east of Broadway. The furrier treated the cap with contempt but gave Seton a dime, on which he survived until he found his Canadian friend a day later.

That winter he made sketches for an advertising firm by day and wrote animal stories at night. In the spring he went back to Manitoba, and over the next decade spent his time in Manitoba, Ontario, New York, Paris and New Mexico before marrying a wealthy woman and settling in New York. By this time he was famous as a naturalist, an illustrator, and a writer of animal stories. The library of his New York home at 144 Fifth Avenue contained a thousand mammal skins and two thousand bird skins along with his photographs, drawings, and detailed journals.

The reading room in the library is the largest room in New York City. A tour guide says softly to a group of visitors that this vast hall, with its rows of long wooden tables under high arched windows, is the size of a football field. The visitors gaze around. Nearly all of them are elderly.

I open the other book in front of me and read that when Sir Charles G.D. Roberts was three, he put his mother's wedding rings around the necks of two dead mice to bring them back to life.

In photographs Sir Charles smiles as often as Michael Snow, which is never. Thin tight lips, face as long as a fiddle, yet from all reports a witty man with a "brilliant social manner" whose rented rooms on West 9th Street were a centre for the New York literati. He dressed the way he did — pince-nez, walking stick, dark suit — in part to confound Americans who thought of Canada as a land of igloos, and perhaps to counter the image of a man who had run away from his wife and children. He left the Maritimes when he was thirty-seven and stayed away a long time.

His animal stories are different from Seton's. They're more focused and less matter-of-fact. Everything is stripped away even as words overaccumulate and lives move irresistably and sadly together. "As the black snake trailed along the winding of the tunnel, his motion made a faint, dry, whispering sound. This delicate sound, together with his peculiar, sickly, elusive scent, travelled just before him, and reached the doorway of the little chamber where the shrew was sleeping."

I suppose it's true that compared to Americans Canadians are sad.

Roberts stayed in New York for eleven years and then went abroad for eighteen more. In North Africa he wrote a story about a New Brunswick snowshoe rabbit, "describing perfectly the cool woodland scenery he had not explored in over a quarter of a century." Both Roberts and Seton blended fiction and natural history, biography and the short story. Seton ended his days in New Mexico, having turned his adobe house into the Seton Institute for the study of nature and Indian lore. Roberts returned to Toronto in 1925. He lived into his eighties — a long life shaped by early memories of animals, and later memories of exile.

• • •

Options. To stay and think about going home, to stay and stop thinking about going home, to go home. Which will it be?

It's six o'clock, and the temperature has dropped. I bring in clothes hardened on the line and place them over the radiator. The smell of cold pours out.

Alec is willing to move to Canada. He says so. But he isn't eager, and we do nothing to advance the move.

"Let Canada come here," he says.

The Third Remove

In countries where the leaves are large as hands
where flowers protrude their fleshy chins
and call their colours
an imaginary snow storm sometimes falls
among the lilies.
And in the early morning one will waken
to think the glowing linen of his pillow
a northern drift, will find himself mistaken
and lie back weeping.

P.K. PAGE
Stories of Snow

Indian Notes

Quiet voice, low-pitched, almost inaudible. "May I have your attention, please? I don't want to make you uncomfortable." More mumblings, then he stops in mid-sentence. For some reason both the woman across from me and I, not having done so to anyone previously, reach out to give him change. We extend our hands to his coffee cup and he doesn't react. Then he moves the cup a few inches towards us. We drop in our coins. His mouth is very dry: he pauses between words, unable to say much or to project.

My destination, mapped out on the subway, is complicated; four changes are required. Each station is stifling, though the trains are cool. I wait in fluorescent darkness, notice the number of white short-sleeved shirts and the cool woman reading on a bench. She reads a dark blue hardback and wears a long cool Indian dress decorated on the bodice with embroidery and tiny mirrors, like the saints in Mexican churches. Someone asks her the time. It's shortly after ten, she answers, and smiles. Her left hand inches down the page as she reads. She seems very calm. At 149th Street she gets off, as do I, and I hope she'll change to the same train — already I imagine a friendship where we pore over *Indian Notes* together — but no, she heads for an uptown train, I a downtown; two stops, then change to the Number 6 going deeper into the Bronx.

The train is almost empty. A skinny woman sits down beside me. "Am I sitting too close?" she asks. I shake my head. She opens and closes a religious tract — *How to Cultivate Christian Manners in an Unmannerly World* — and underlines sections. Some paragraphs are scored through with pink felt pen, certain lines are underscored with ballpoint. She circles *All* in *Well-Mannered at All Times*. Then underlines *Well-*

Mannered. She seems doped up and twitchy, and I'm glad when she gets off.

The train empties of its few people at Castle Hill Avenue. I ride alone to Zerega Avenue. No one gets on. Then, just before the doors close, someone does: a young man, very wild and shabby. He sits across from me, down a little. When he speaks to me — asks me the time — my mouth is dry. He speaks to me again, something about talking to people on the subway: he likes to, most people don't. I smile a little as he talks, make eye contact yet don't, try to look friendly, not too friendly, not too afraid, and my vagina seems to loosen, get wet, with fear.

I get out at my stop, walk down the steps into Westchester Square, find the library set back behind a peeling wrought-iron fence and shaded by trees: Huntington Free Library and Reading Room, by appointment only. I ring the bell and walk into an earlier time: long dark wooden tables, wooden bookshelves, antique typewriters on top of the card catalogue, fans in the high vaulted ceiling: quiet, breeze, smell of books. As I fill out slips, my hand still trembles.

A small bell hangs on a post. A sign asks you to ring the bell to get one of the librarians to come. Another sign says, GUARD DOG ON DUTY. PLEASE DO NOT GO BEYOND THIS POINT. The volumes of *Indian Notes* are the size of hymnals, small and easy to hold, the covers well-maintained but slightly faded — a dark red. I read about the beaver bundle of Mad-Wolf, a collection of powerful medicinal objects wrapped inside a beaver skin, "in importance and sacredness surpassed by none."

The Blackfeet, to whom Mad-Wolf belonged, used to range from the Northern Saskatchewan River in Alberta to the Yellowstone River in Montana, and from the Rockies to the Missouri River. The last major plague of smallpox came by way of a Missouri River steamboat in 1869; the last of the great herds of buffalo was annihilated in 1883; the last large numbers of Blackfeet starved to death in the winter and spring of 1884. They sold vast tracts of land to the United States and "now occupy only a narrow strip of country bordering upon the eastern slopes of the northern Rockies." I ring the small bell. A librarian brings out McClintock's *The Old North Trail*, published in 1910, and I read it the way someone in wartime reads about peace and tranquillity. He names the plants he sees as he follows his Blackfoot friend to his encampment, meets Mad-Wolf, and is adopted into the tribe.

Untie the beaver bundle — spread it open to reveal the skins of many birds and animals. Hold up the beaver skin, move it in imitation of the animal's swimming. Place dried grass on live coals, and in that atmosphere of smoke and fragrance, pray for protection from sickness and danger.

Manhattan Rain

Rain slides down over nectarines, lemons, my ankles. I step back into the fragrance of mango under an awning — skin beaten soft with rain, rain fragrant with fruit. It's the first time all day I've been outside: a lull in the rain which soon recommences and harder than ever.

I buy bananas and wait. Several others gather under the awning: a woman who bites her fingers and in the process conceals most of her face with her hand, an older man in a blue shirt, a much older woman who touches grapes as she talks about them. We look out at the rain.

A slender woman with long thick hair walks by under an umbrella. We smile at each other and she walks on — sandals, bare legs, a light step — a remarkable composure for a woman whose child has just died. I've met her twice, once in Theresa's apartment and once in the doctor's office, her baby a month old, as was mine. She was radiant with the fact of her child whom she bounced on her knee. "She loves the new African jazz," she said. "I put it on at night and dance with her and she just goes down into it," and her hand swept low in a deep curve. Sleep was the thread of our conversation. Her daughter slept, my son didn't.

The second time I saw her, I didn't recognize her. It was four months later and she was without her baby. She arrived at Theresa's with a bag of baby clothing she wanted to return. The baby would never fit the clothes, she said, and therefore it was better not to have them around. She had had experience, she explained, with this sort of thing. Only a year before she had moved in with a friend whose baby was dying. She knew everything that had to be done.

After she left, Theresa explained that she had wanted a baby for years and finally convinced her husband to have one, only for it to be born with a rare disease: its muscles would progressively degenerate and within the year it would die.

As she went by in the rain, I was holding my few purchases with one hand and Ben, nearly eighteen months old, in the crook of my arm. She smiled, recognizing me before I recognized her as she had in Theresa's apartment — "We were at the doctor's the same day," she said, and immediately I remembered — her smile a genuine one and her greatest protection — she used it to hold people at bay. She didn't break stride but simply smiled and walked on.

Sad onion rain. In a Cree tale, a man watches young girls in the spring rub wild onions under their eyes until tears come out, and he calls those tears sad onion rain.

When Hannah's baby died in New York City on February 28, 1863, they took the body by boat to New London, Connecticut and buried him in the Groton cemetery. That was Hannah's first winter in this country. Charles Hall had brought her from Cumberland Sound along with her husband and their baby to help raise money for another of his arctic expeditions.

For a few days one of their two sled-dogs escaped and roamed the streets of New York. By spring both dogs had died. A whaling captain offered to take the two homesick

Inuit north, but Hall wouldn't allow it. He moved them into his furnished rooms and they all lived there through the summer and autumn of 1863 — trapped in the heat and claustrophobia and sickness of New York City.

Under the awning, we continued to wait for the rain to stop. The woman who bit her fingers lowered her hand and her profile was more ravaged, less pretty, than I expected. She seemed to look at me as often as I looked at her, and I tried to pace my glances. She was dressed in light blue and her face looked chalky. I looked up again, trying to put my finger on it, and she was gone. Had she been crying?

Then I saw that she wasn't gone. She had moved back into the shop as had three of the other customers: the man in the blue shirt, the old woman, and an old man.

The rain slowed and the man in the blue shirt headed out, and she behind him, opening her umbrella under the awning. As she moved beside him, I realized they were together. She held the umbrella over both of them and directed a smile at the man who was only interested in the rain.

When Hall first brought Hannah and her family to New York in 1862, he put them on display at P.T. Barnum's Museum. Another Canadian was on display at the same time: Anna Swan, the seven foot six inch giantess from Mill Brook, Nova Scotia. When the museum caught fire in 1865, Anna was found nearly unconscious on the third floor. According to the *New York Tribune*, "her best friend, the living skeleton, stood by her as long as he dared, but then deserted her, while perspiration rolled from her face in little brooks and rivulets which pattered musically upon the floor." Too large to go through doors, too heavy to be taken down the stairs, she had to be trussed up with a rope, lifted by a derrick through a large hole in the wall and "swung over the heads of the people in the street, with eighteen men grasping the other extremity of the line."

On an overseas tour she met her husband, Martin Van

Buren Bates, the Kentucky giant. They were presented to Queen Victoria (just as Hannah and her husband had been), and travelled throughout Europe. Anna gave birth to two children, both abnormally large, who died within hours of being born. Two days before her forty-second birthday, she died of TB.

Hannah died of TB. Both of her children died very young. Even her adopted daughter died before she did. When Hannah died, she was thirty-eight.

• • •

Cool: the area next to the Hudson River; the aura around a flower; the area around this desk.

Yesterday *Annie Hall* was on in the video store. I watched the scene where Alvy Singer brings Marshall McLuhan out from behind the movie placard.

In the library the man beside me wears gloves and spreads sections of newspaper all around him taking up nearly the whole table; an aggressive "crazy" rustle. The woman across from me has telltale lips — lipstick applied wide of the mark — and angry eyes that concentrate on a piece of yellow paper which she folds and adds to her collection of envelopes. Now she licks a stamp.

In this quiet place craziness comes. She takes out a legal-size yellow pad, the kind Gould used, and like him writes without putting down the date.

I look out the window and see Gould walking — a homeless man, blanket around his shoulders despite the warmth. Gould was picked up in Florida where he was sitting, dressed as usual, on a park bench. The police didn't want his overdressed presence to give the city a bad name.

Why is the image of warm clothing so moving? Gould — in hat, gloves, coat and muffler — in the middle of summer. In the middle of Manhattan.

The Inuit sea goddess Sedna married a fulmar, grey sea

bird of the petrel family, who promised her a tent made of beautiful skins and clothes made of bird feathers. "You shall rest on soft bearskins," he told her. She went with him and discovered that his house was wretched.

The next summer her father rescued her: he killed the bird, took Sedna into his boat, and set off for home. In revenge, the birds stirred up a storm and Sedna's practical father threw her overboard. She clung to the edge of the boat while he chopped off her fingers, joint by joint, down to the stumps — the first joints swam away as whales, the second joints as seals, the stumps as ground seals. (Gould, in fingerless gloves, playing the ivories.)

In 1976 his fingers lost their facility and for a year he didn't play. On notepads he documented the progression of his troubles, the depth of his anxiety. His physical ills were interspersed with weather reports — the temperature of Timmins, and his own.

McLuhan spent a year in New York from 1967 to 1968. The blackouts he had suffered since the fifties got worse. He was finally persuaded to see a doctor, and tests revealed a tumour as big as a tennis ball under his brain. He refused surgery until doctors raised the spectre of blindness and insanity.

The operation at Columbia Presbyterian lasted seventeen hours. His brain had to be lifted up to get at the tumour, and the doctor took fifteen minutes to plot out each cut. In time the pain lessened but his senses remained raw. "He seemed to be one exposed and quivering nerve," his biographer writes. "Entering the kitchen of his own home was like stepping into a chemical factory. Noise particularly tormented him. When planes flew over his house in Bronxville, McLuhan literally screamed in agony."

The operation jarred his personality and his memory. He became more erratic, abusive, inflexible; "several years of reading got rubbed out," while forgotten memories returned.

He rediscovered a childhood love for the music of Harry Lauder, the Scottish tenor whose records Robert Flaherty took up to Hudson Bay when he made his film *Nanook of the North.*

Gould liked Canada and McLuhan detested it. Before leaving New York, McLuhan did an interview with *Mademoiselle* in which he described the Canadian character. English Canada was "the most apathetic and unenthusiastic territory in all creation . . . The Canadian is mildewed with caution."

Gould and McLuhan knew each other. They were neighbours for a while and fond of each other. Both loved to talk, though in different ways, and both courted celebrity, in different ways. Gould was a private man and McLuhan a public man. Both were defined by hot and cold: the pianist who went to such lengths to stay warm while remaining fascinated by the north, and the philosopher who constructed a terminology based on temperature: radio was hot, television was cool; books were hot, bull sessions were cool.

Gould thought of cold in the old sense, the Greek sense, of a living being or entity: the cold, the hot, the wet, the dry. Like Joyce Wieland, he was fascinated by maps of the north and pored over them in school. Below a certain latitude he became profoundly depressed. "It really had something to do," he said, "with the quality of the light, with the sudden fadeouts at night, for example."

Gould couldn't understand McLuhan's idea that television was cool and radio hot; surely it was the other way around. And he confessed to "the sneaking suspicion that Marshall doesn't listen to that much radio, frankly."

Gould listened to radio twenty-four hours a day. Wallpaper, he called it. Even while he slept, the radio was on, and so he would wake knowing things but not knowing how he knew them.

In Gould all my fascinations coalesce: the notion of hot

and cold as entities, of fur and snow as a tangible expression of those two forces. The small oriental rug at his feet — furs to China — embodies the longing for Cathay that unlocked a snowy country and led by indirect trade routes back to China.

• • •

Summer-coolness. The pillowcase is cool, the sheet is cool. Much cooler than in winter when the windows are closed. Night air has been stirring, and now I put my hand on this fresh new temperature and move my cheek over to the new air resting on the pillow.

Ben wakes between us — warmth of his cheek, little hands. He comes with me into the kitchen. The floor is cool. My feet get cooler, the floor no warmer. Sochi comes into the kitchen — warm body in a thin cotton slip.

We make coffee. "Hot!" to Ben. "Hot!" "Haw," he says back.

In winter, cold is blasted away by heat or heat gradually dispelled, but never this fluidity — one temperature moving through another.

The Dilemma of Being Canadian

All my thoughts are on Canada, the chief anchor in my life, which means I'm anchored to something falling apart. Anchored to a private notion at odds with reality. That's why it's unsettling to meet other English Canadians. We should have so much in common but don't.

I was standing next to the glass display case in the consulate. Behind me a voice asked, "Is your book there?"

"No," I said, "Is yours?"

"I thought it would be," he said, "but it's not." And then, "Are you a Canadian? Do you live here? How long have you lived here? What do you do here?"

I said, "What do *you* do here?"

I knew his name by then. We had shaken hands, though I refrained from saying I was a writer, and even longer from saying I was writing about Canadians in New York. (Here I was with a real live Canadian and I couldn't get away fast enough.) When I did tell him, he said something interesting. He said that every Canadian has an internal vision of the world in which the upper part is a wide horizontal snowy plane with a solitary figure on the horizon. "Do you think that's right?" he asked me. It sounded good to me. "What does the rest of the world look like?" But he didn't have a picture for that.

We shook hands goodbye. "I think we're glad to have met each other," he said, and his smile was amused and unconvinced. He bent down to kiss my cheek.

"I kissed your earring," he said.

Oh. So then I kissed his cheek, but my kiss also landed on bony ground.

My image of the north is of two bands: the lower one occupied by concrete and fields, the upper band story-filled and out of bounds. For years I had the feeling that it would be discourteous — poaching — to use Inuit and Indian stories. Less so, the stories of explorers, though even that was suspect, subject to putdown.

English Canadians have a strange stance towards our colonizing, colonized past. A stance so reserved as to appear only indifferent and hostile, when, in fact, other strands are at play. The courtesy, I've mentioned; some guilt, loneliness. Mostly ignorance. Native stories seem much more a part of my world when I'm away from Canada. Is that because I'm too far away to be scolded?

At the consulate I asked for names of other Canadians in New York, asked what sort of book they would be interested in reading. Their ideas dissipated mine and mine bored them. Peter Jennings, they said, Ken Taylor. If you want the book to be published here, it will have to deal with Canadians that Americans can recognize.

Later, sitting across from the pretzel man on the corner of 50th Street and 6th Avenue, I wrote in my notebook: Dilemma. The more I address the subject the more it falls away.

• • •

Mirrors, so old and tarnished they have the texture of cloth. Chandeliers. The roundabout voice of Graham Fraser. I climb up the stairs, red-carpeted, soft, to the open banquet room at the top. The man beside me introduces himself: so and so from Avon products.

Graham Fraser is explaining that Canada comes from a private and European tradition without the big monuments that tell the story of American history. Americans have solved their problems with arms; Canadians with constitutional conferences. He calls the breakup of Canada "almost a Greek tragedy: a blend of inevitability and pride flowing from a misunderstanding."

The men in suits stare off into space. Maybe they're listening more than they appear to be, but I doubt it. They perk up when a British reporter — clipped, precocious, impatient — starts to talk. He wants Quebec to separate. He's champing at the bit for the other regions to follow suit. He talks about western Canada's true interests lying south of the border, suggests it makes complete sense for them to join the United States, pretends to champion the fringes of the country against the squat power of Ontario while delivering the country — in parts — to the United States.

Fraser sees a different future. He sees parts of Canada begging to join the United States and being turned down.

• • •

Linda Bouchard composes music in a single room across the street. Like Lévi-Strauss (in New York with other refugees in the early forties) asking Darius Milhaud when he realized he was going to be a composer, I ask Linda — "When did you realize?" And the answers are strikingly similar, and even more strikingly different.

She answers that at seventeen "before going to sleep, I had this urge to write music," even though she didn't hear any music in her head or even know how to write music down. She remembers feeling so incompetent that she cried.

Milhaud answered that when he was a child slowly falling asleep, he was listening and hearing music different from any he knew; "he discovered later that this was already his own music."

Linda — not till seventeen, and then no actual sounds, just the desire. But both — before falling asleep.

She grew up in Montreal, one of fourteen children whose parents knew nothing of music. She is in her early thirties now, with short black hair turning silver above silver earrings: a fine-metal radiance around her ears.

She wants a back yard and garden. After more than ten years in New York, the last six in a single room, she thinks about Canada a lot: "the space, the cold, not desolate but stark, there is no extra."

But when she goes back she feels again the claustrophobia: "the world ends with Quebec, or starts outside Quebec. If you don't learn another language you're stuck in Quebec, but if you learn another language you're betraying Quebec, and they never let you back in. That's how it feels."

"You can go to France," she says, "but that's even more of a betrayal. I would rather learn English than speak that kind of French."

Her work has been performed in the United States, France, English Canada, but never Montreal. Never her home town. "I've sent them things," she says, "but they've always found reasons to say no." She talks about going to the Radio-Canada studio in New York to be interviewed on the English side, and made to feel absolutely uncomfortable by two journalists on the French side. "You're in New York? And we don't know you!"

That's where she met Maurice. "Thank God he came in," she says.

These new friendships don't develop. In the beginning I feel such pleasure to have met someone from Quebec and entered Canada without entering Canada — entered a new world which is also home — but the friendships don't develop. New York is too big perhaps. Our paths don't naturally cross. And perhaps we're too different, after all.

I meet Michele, a bold, funny, beautifully dressed young woman who wears a strand of pearls. Over our bowls of soup, she tells me that soon I'll be able to move to Montreal. "In a few years Quebec is going to be an independent country, and you'll be able to move there and be accepted just like any other foreigner."

She has long arms and lean white expressive hands the colour of the almonds I'm peeling for dinner. Her face is pretty, younger than mine by ten years. She is alone in New York, studying. In a year she'll go back to Montreal.

I tell her that if I were from Quebec I would probably want to separate but I'm from Ontario, and so it makes me sad.

"What makes you sad?"

"The idea of the country falling apart."

"You want to enclose us," she says. "No one in Quebec feels that way."

She says, "You don't know much. You're willing to learn, but you don't know about Quebec."

I think of saying, you don't know about Canada, we don't know about each other. But I lose my forthrightness in her company.

Boston Corners

For a time I used to write letters, hurry to mail them, and immediately upon mailing be overwhelmed by the belief, the certainty, that I had repeated myself: much of what I had written I had written one letter back. The friend would receive the letter and think, how little she attends to me, she has already told me these things before. And in the next letter I might ask, "Do I repeat myself?" The feeling was of sending myself only to cancel myself out.

A package arrives from home — a roll of newspaper articles so battered en route they arrive in a post office envelope marked RECEIVED IN DAMAGED CONDITION. Pages torn from the *Globe and Mail*, the *London Free Press*, *Maclean's*. My mother's reused stamps on the torn brown wrapping are a thirty-nine cent Canadian flag and a five cent Lievre d'Amerique/Varying Hare.

The article from *Maclean's* is about the possibility of union with the United States. "Do Canadians and Americans want to meet a new millenium as one nation?" A photograph shows the six-metre-wide swath through the forest that marks the 49th parallel, and the article details poll after poll: Do Canadians want to join the U.S.? Do Americans want us to join? Do Canadians prefer Bush to Mulroney?

I ask four American friends if they know what the 49th parallel is and none of them does.

It's mid-July and the heat doesn't ease at night. At seven in the morning the apartment is stuffy despite ceiling fans: heat has accumulated for weeks, talk drifts inside. Periodically throughout the night, and from six in the morning on, we could be in someone else's living room.

On Saturday morning we drive north along the east side of the Hudson River for two and a half hours. Away from the main highway the roads are lined with wild flowers: chicory, yarrow, black-eyed Susans, Queen Anne's Lace. Everything is warm and plentiful. The hills are rolling, the roadsides are wild gardens, the houses are graceful and cool. Such northern lushness fills these southernmost reaches of the north that I murmur to Alec how beautiful it is, nowhere is Canada so soft and abundant.

We take Highway 22, and there — jumping out at us from around a curve — is a sign, *Boston Corners*. "Take it," I say. "Turn left." And so, having wanted to see it, not knowing where exactly it was, we come upon it — the village where David Milne lived and painted. A few houses — which house was his? — and the beautifully treed hills beyond.

Milne was twenty-two when he left Paisley, Ontario for New York City. He attended the Art Students League, and became one of the circle of visitors to 291 Fifth Avenue, Alfred Stieglitz's first gallery: "In those little rooms, under the skylights, we met Cézanne, Van Gogh, Gauguin, Matisse, Picasso, Brancusi. For the first time we saw courage and imagination bare, not sweetened by sentiment and smothered in technical skill."

Fourteen years later, in 1916, he and his wife moved from New York to Boston Corners. They found a vacant frame house a quarter of a mile from the road and rented it for six dollars a month. They cooked on a stone fireplace in the back yard and "life then was almost all in the open. We paid little attention to the house, except when it rained."

He painted scenes close by, walking two miles or less, painting on the spot, finishing on the spot; "good or bad, they were left alone." To friends in New York he wrote walking letters. "The Spring. Small drink, religious observance merely, not thirsty. Off again to have another look at those fog banks from the top . . . Coming along the top noticed the metallic smell of the overripe huckleberries . . . I am writing this on a rock in the middle of the larger stream above the junction."

He scouted the bush and chose a site for his painting hut

close to a stream. He built the hut in the fall of 1920 and in January moved in. A photograph shows him in the doorway in suit and tie, hands in his pockets, jacket spread open at the waist, his head all but invisible. He seems to be wearing a wide-brimmed hat.

His painting, *From the Doorway, Alander Cabin*, February 12, 1921, shows the inside of the cabin: the frypan on the stove, the chair, box, and table, the two windows and the open door, and beyond them birch trees and snow. Light penetrates portions of the room and touches "the stove with its rusty vermilions, greys, blues and purples . . . as brilliant as an orchid."

There's something we learn as children: it's easier to be homesick than to be happy at home.

It's Saturday afternoon, Alec has taken the kids to Central Park, I'm alone — reading David Milne's letters. He went back to Canada but not because he missed it. The place he missed after he left it was Boston Corners.

Milne felt less Canadian than Scottish. I feel Canadian, though it's a feeling dissipated by meeting other Canadians. I'm more comfortable meeting people from Quebec who don't feel Canadian at all.

Rain. Faint but steady smell of garbage through the open window.

He writes, " . . . at the door, again impressed and delighted with the recurring miracle of the untouched hut — the ham on the stove (I almost expected to find it still bubbling), the evaporated milk in the jelly jar with the tea tin over it, the pile of bedding with the hollow I had made in it Sunday night before we left. The contrast between my own fussy wanderings and the serene unchangeableness of the hut never fails to hit me hard — it alone is worth a three mile climb . . . "

The image of a cabin with an open door puts a face on my longings and shapes everything I see, so that the dim light in this apartment reminds me of a cabin in the rain, and the street outside is an absence of trees, and the darkness at night is the darkness of a stage set: a heavy, artificial, heightened atmosphere — murky, intriguing, unnatural. Light doesn't spread out but remains in pockets surrounded by darkness — streetlights with highrises on either side.

We came home last night and heard shouting before we turned the corner. The road was blocked by a car and by three screaming people pounding on it. The car door opened and two men spilled out, one with a baseball bat. He raised it and the other man pulled him back. A young kid flew at him. "What's he doing?" Alec said, "he's half the size of the other guy!"

But "he" was a woman, a skinny, short-cropped woman who flew at the man again and got shoved back. The car sped off, its wheels crunching over broken glass.

I always look first to see if my desk is untouched. I listen for any noise, then look around the door and down the full dark length of the apartment.

• • •

Alec dreams about his father. He looks outside and his father is in the garden pruning trees. Alec thinks, we have to be careful not to scare him off, and he goes to the door and says quietly, why don't you come inside. His father comes in and is delighted to see everyone. They talk for some time.

We enter the field where the Alander Mountain Trail begins, and my thoughts are full of David Milne and of how preposterous our climb is going to be, weighed down as we are with parcels of food, strings of sleeping bags, odd-shaped bundles. We walk through pasture: wild strawberry, Scotch burr, clover, butter and eggs — a reflecting pool in the distance, easily one of the ones he painted — then into woods, an abandoned house, wild blackberries, a stream, and then gradually uphill, the trail muddy where narrow and low, dry where wide and higher, until we reach our spot: a campsite next to Ashley Hill Brook. We pitch our tent under trees next to a rapids — a gulch between hills — David Milne country.

I go back alone to get another load from the car and see the wide-brimmed hat, slender build, cleanshaven face, as he stops to sip from an earlier, cleaner stream, "religious observance merely."

Near here he painted *Black Rapids, Pool and Contours, Copake Ravine, Cooking in the Woods, The Open Stream.* He was happier than he had ever been, or would be again, at least in a general way. He was always puzzled about why they had to leave.

Cooler last night. Alec's tears against my cheek. It's different from anything he has felt before, he says, the way it permeates everything.

After his father died, we all went out into the garden and spread his ashes over the grass. The kids too, who didn't know the significance and thought it was some kind of game. They fought with each other over who was getting the most handfuls and almost upset the box. The whole thing was a blend of the sad and knowing, the comic and unknowing. But Alec wanted something more.

This morning he bathed in the brook. He lay down in a foot of icy water to get his circulation going, he said, then made coffee over the fire, nursing the blaze until the water boiled; he added generous spoonfuls of espresso and stirred, then poured the frothy brew through a coffee sock into cups and added cream kept cool in the brook.

The woods are full of mushrooms of brilliant colours and great variety. Full of flowers — tall and tight, or short and loose, but nearly all white and star-shaped. It is a navigable woods, paths lead through it, and the trees are widely spaced.

In the afternoon we find a muddy road and follow it. Alec carries Sochi down the middle of the road, I walk with the baby through long grass and brush off to the left. He makes better progress.

"I learned so much in Guatemala," he says when I catch up with him.

"Like what?"

"Like how to walk down a muddy road."

He talks about measurements used in the Guatemalan countryside: the *cuerda* which is a little less than an acre, the *barra* a little less than a yard — the distance from fingertips to elbow of one of the kings of France. The *legua*, or league. From the spot where Alec lived to the nearest store was eight leagues.

It was when we were swimming the next day that I remembered his comment about learning how to learn by watching people. "In Guatemala," he said, "you watch someone do something and then you do it. There's not a lot of talk." I was watching him in the water with Sochi — his unfailing patience, her delight.

Once, after a long bad day with her, I asked him what I should do.

"Discover more patience," he answered.

"Where can I discover patience?"

He laughed. "In your heart." Tapping his.

In my heart.

His long arms reached for her, much longer from fingertips to elbow than a *barra*, but a measurement unfamiliar to me even so. A *cuerda* of love?

Now, for the third time, I read to Sochi "the part where Tootles shoots Wendy with an arrow." Each stage of the story ripples across her face: the drama of Wendy falling to the ground, the enormity of Tootles's mistake, Peter's arrival, his confusion, his anger, and then his discovery that the acorn he had given to Wendy for a kiss — not knowing what "kiss" meant — has deflected the arrow and saved her life.

This is like Neverland, I tell her. These woods. I wonder if Peter Pan is here. But she will have none of that.

I keep trying to get to the end of *Peter Pan* but Sochi wants me to reread: Tootles and the arrow; the mermaids' lagoon. She doesn't want the goodbyes.

On the way back to New York, we drive through Boston Corners again. There must be more to it, I think, another road. But no. Boston Corners has dwindled since Milne lived here. The railway station has gone, the church, the store, a number of houses it seems. And no one is around to tell us anything: we stop at the Old Homestead Bar and it's closed. Alec notices a lone gas pump surrounded by grass in front of a barn: Chevron Supreme. A golf course occupies what must have been woods, and on a side road a few people sell the golf balls they've scavenged.

This Question of Missing

Borduas was very much alone when he lived in New York because he spoke almost no English, and yet he thrived. His style of painting changed radically, and his output was prodigious.

He came here, sick and discouraged, in 1953. His "Refus Global," urging personal liberation from a society defined by Catholicism and capitalism, from "a colony trapped within the slippery walls of fear," had enraged the Quebec government, foreshadowed Quebec's Quiet Revolution, and cost him his job; he was fired from the École du Meuble. Over the next three years he became increasingly poor. He developed serious ulcers, his wife and three children left him, he scarcely painted.

In New York he blossomed. He lived at 119 East 17th Street, "a beautiful studio," he said, "huge, very bright, and all white." He switched from paintbrush to palette knife and concentrated on light: "my painting is becoming more and

more 'transparent' perhaps? More crystalline in any case."
His financial worries continued, "yet I am sustained by an
unshakeable and unjustified hope. I paint huge pictures
which look like balloons seeking freedom, suddenly released
from my hopes."

After two years in New York he continued his journey of
exile to Paris where his exhilaration changed to homesickness, and his paintings became simpler, more arresting, even
more beautiful. He spent five years in Paris and they were the
last five years of his life. Not long before he died, he was
making plans to go back to Quebec. He wrote a childhood
friend about building a studio on the Richelieu River between
St. Mathias and St. Hilaire where he was born.

The paintings of this period, when "I would give all the
blessings of the earth for a small corner were it in Canada,"
are often black and white: ragged, raven-like flaps of black lie
between thick, almost sculpted, white.

The image of Borduas crosses in my mind with the image
of a homesick Emily Carr. In London, in 1902, she suffered
from headaches, weeping, numbness, stuttered speech. She
entered a sanatorium and for fifteen months was treated for
hysteria with electric massage and "heavy feeding." She didn't
recover until she went home.

Eight years later, at the age of thirty-eight, she went to Paris
with her sister. After three months, she began to feel herself
going "as I had in London." She spent twelve weeks in the
hospital, then came back to her room and discovered that if
she perched a chair on the chest of drawers she could see a
garden below. She spent hours in that precarious spot looking down at trees and grass.

Her childhood was shaped by her mother's illness (she died
of tuberculosis when Emily was fourteen), and by intimacy
with her father. She had been his favourite, and then their
mutual affection went sour. He became for her "a cross, gouty
sexy old man who hurt and disgusted me." Having been

raised by a man against whom she rebelled, and by an older sister who thrashed her until she fainted, she found in Indian villages a sensibility entirely lacking in her family: a looseness, a fluidity, a transparency between nature and self. Her life, punctuated by travels which were punctuated by breakdowns, became a tale of captivity and escape — into woods, animals, Indian life. She made of retreat something aggressive, wounded, peaceful and new.

The year before he died, Borduas wrote about his idea of home and how it had changed. Initially he belonged, he said, first to his village and then to his province. "I considered myself French-Canadian." After his first trip to Europe, he considered himself more Canadian than French. In New York, "merely Canadian, just like my compatriots." In Paris he thought of himself as North American. He spoke, depending upon the translation, of a lyrical and virginal "greenness" or "freshness" in relation to North America. That was what he missed more than anything else.

"So why didn't he go back?" a friend asks me. The question has never occurred to me. Such a simple, obvious question. Why not? If he missed it so much.

These voluntary exiles are troublesome. People are puzzled by them and not necessarily sympathetic. They wonder how true the missing is.

The missing is true. It seems like the only true thing. I suppose we find it easier to miss than to go back and risk not liking what we thought we missed. I survive in New York by missing Canada. Most New Yorkers have some shield they erect between themselves and the city. This is mine.

New York gives me Canada in a way that is more vivid, more sentimental, than Canada gives me itself. It gives me the emotional Canada that's so hard to find when you're there.

The Fourth Remove

He spoke of it gently as a foreign land to which he would never now be able to return. It touched my imagination so that I began to regard the city of Las Casas hidden there in the mountains at the end of a mule track, with only one rough road running south, as the real object of my journey — and the beginning of going home.

GRAHAM GREENE
The Lawless Roads

The Snow Was Burning

We drove under a moon the colour of light orange wax. I remembered the story of the moon beaten about the face with a rabbit, and the long grey shapes that remained on the wallpaper when we took our wet bathing suits off the hooks. The wallpaper was purple, rose, and grey; our damp shadows had long ears. They listened and remembered a time of easy talk between many things: animals and people, hot and cold, wet and dry.

The moon was beaten about the face with a rabbit for being hesitant. In Aztec mythology, it rose so waveringly into the sky that the gods grew angry and punished it. The shape of the rabbit is visible in the moon's face, our rabbit selves were visible on the wall, the moon bears the scars of hesitation, the wall the loss of our listening selves.

Our shadows on the wall were cool. In the heat of this new and dying age, they were all that was cool. They dried and left a slight stain on the wallpaper, grey scar on the moon.

It never gets cool now, not even at night.

One summer it got so hot that everyone forgot their names. They couldn't remember who they were. For a time they looked for their names but soon they forgot to do even that. They just sat still.

One person had a rocking chair. She rocked until she fell asleep. In her dream, Canada and cool made the same sound.

Each person in turn sat in the rocking chair, each person dreamed a name and on waking told what it was. All the names were variations of cool. Siberia Cool, Pelly Cool, Inuvik Cool. In this way they were all named again.

One woman wanted a name for her newborn child. She thought of Snow. North. Marten. Loon. She got out the atlas and it fell open not at a map but at a section called Polar

Regions, under the larger heading of The Diversity of Life. She read that tundra is land from which the ice retreated eight thousand years ago. Tundra remembers the ice: it has only a thin covering of soil. A burn victim remembers the fire.

She dreamt about snow, and then dreamt the snow was burning.

• • •

In the subway he stands very thin by the door between trains, whispering. He holds a handkerchief to his throat, then lowers the handkerchief to reveal the hole in his windpipe.

I look down at my book and read Lévi-Strauss's words: "What meaning can be attributed to the strange conception of a call coming from a vegetable or mineral entity that has no power of articulate expression?"

His throat is darkskinned and narrow. "The gentle call of a rotten tree." Only the removal of the handkerchief makes his message clear.

I change trains. In the station a heavyset Mexican bends over a plastic tray on which he carefully lines up bags of cashews. He flattens them as he lines them up, fitting "bricks" for the bag above. No one is buying.

In the beginning, according to one South American myth, people lived underground and from time to time they heard the cry of a savannah bird. One day some men followed the sound. They came to a hole and climbed up through it onto the earth's surface where they found "great quantities of fruit, bees and honey, and they noticed also dead trees and dry wood." They brought back samples of everything to their ancestor, Kaboi, who "concluded that the earth was a beautiful and fertile place, but that the presence of dead wood proved that everything was doomed to perish."

The hole was a wound, a neutral territory presided over by a white handkerchief as the man surrendered again and again to our lack of attention. His whisper followed us as we travelled through a long horizontal shaft up into a city of rotten wood, corruption, "everything doomed to perish."

Theresa won't come here. She finds it too painful to see all the stolen objects in the museum and know that the people to whom they belong have nothing. I nod, agree, can't really explain the joy I feel when I'm here, the relief to be in the presence of cultures other than this one.

Ornament made of beetle wing covers and toucan feathers. Bracelet of armadillo shell worn by girls. Back ornament made of oilbird bones, whole birdskins, and beetle wing covers.

My hand holds leaking coffee, a paper cup stealthily hidden in my purse. My fingers smell of coffee, as does my pen.

"Around the time of puberty, children may receive their new, adult names, sometimes during ritual ear or lip piercing."

Ritual holes, decorated escape routes. I walk through the beautiful narrow passageways lined with exhibits behind glass: marten against an Oregon backdrop; wolverine, fifty miles northeast of Snowbird Lake in the Northwest Territories; wolves running over snow in pursuit of a deer — giant grey shapes going full tilt three feet away.

On the fifth floor, large windows provide a view of the greenish metallic rooftops of other parts of the Museum of Natural History, Central Park just beyond. This is where you can pore over well-thumbed catalogues and trace the stories of the artifacts downstairs.

16.1/555. Haida house post about ten feet high purchased at $1.00 per foot from Alfred Adams of Masset via Prince Rupert, British Columbia by Harlan I. Smith. It was one of the first two house posts seen after passing the old grave going towards the ocean at Yan.

16.1/557a. Haida totem pole about twenty-four feet long

purchased at $1.00 per foot from Alfred Adams . . . It was one of two next towards the ocean from where 555 and 556 stood. Because it wasn't carved, the top was cut off and left behind while the rest of the pole was sent to New York.

In the accession envelope is the correspondence between Harlan I. Smith, the museum anthropologist, and Alfred Adams, the Indian in Masset who acted as his "exporter." An old faded postcard wrapped in soft white paper shows Alfred Adams, Henry Edenshaw, Reverend William Hogan, Indian agent Thomas Deasy, and Douglas Edenshaw standing at the base of what is probably a totem pole, hard to say. The surface of the picture has gone glittery with age, silvery-metallic.

A letter from Alfred Adams sent from Masset on April 28th, 1910 is addressed to H.I. Smith Esq, Central Park, New York. "My dear Sir. I am enclosing you the tracts of all your money I hope you will content with it, I did my very best to cut the expences small." Adams spent five days and used five men at twenty-five cents an hour to crate up four totem poles and ship them out by boat. Smith wrote back that he wanted more house posts, and specified that the poles should not be "over eighteen feet high or twenty-seven and a half inches wide"; otherwise they wouldn't fit in the hall.

The hall is the Northwest Coast hall downstairs, the most beautiful room in New York. Totem poles rise up to the ceiling in the dusky light of a museum preserving its treasures. Twelve poles mark off a central passageway on either side of which cherry-wood cabinets hold smaller objects: tarnished silver bracelets engraved with Haida designs, softened shredded cedarbark lined with fur, grease dishes so impregnated with oil they still shine.

In the great green room there was a telephone and a red balloon — the words from last night's bedtime story with "its courtly order/its list of farewells/to everything." To my left, Tsimshian shamanistic regalia, and in the case: 16.1/883, "neck ring of cedarbark." In my notes I've written down the collector's original description: "Neck girdle of red cedar bark hung with the skins of a hawk, a kingfisher, a flicker and a snipe's wing, and the head and wing of a small species of hawk. This assists the shaman in his movements about the sick."

Two of the totem poles, too tall to be erected in full, have been cut in half and the halves erected. Another pole is from Bella Coola, "purchased at $10.00, crating $5.00 through Mr. John Clayton, from south side of River. Eagle horizontal on top." Others are from Comox, Neweltee, Ft. Rupert, Clayoquath, Koskimo, Masset, "purchased at $1.00 per foot."

The newspaper has stories about flower wars and slain children: four children in nine days have been killed by stray bullets; the owners of flower shops are going to the police to get rid of unlicensed vendors, most of them Mexican, who push shopping carts full of roses, mums and gladiolas through the streets. The vendors get forty percent of as little as seventy dollars a day, working as they do for other vendors, and each time they're arrested their carts are thrown away and they're put in jail for up to five days.

In March of 1989, Jim Thunder came in person to tell the museum that Big Bear's power bundle was homesick. The bundle contains a grizzly bear paw, sweetgrass, and tobacco wrapped inside ten cloths, the innermost one a small floral print in pink and blue. The bundle is in storage and has never been displayed. The museum tag says, "Plains Cree Medicine Bundle 50.2 — 3739 A-M said to have belonged to Big Bear."

Jim Thunder isn't popular here. The archivist who brings me the file says, "You'll find a lot of people didn't like Jim Thunder any more than we did." The file contains letters from other Cree who dispute his claim to be Big Bear's adopted great-great-grandson. A phone call from Winnipeg is reported: the woman says Thunder "slept with everybody across Canada" and urges the museum to discount his 2,700-

mile run from Edmonton to New York, a run inspired by a
ten-year-old dream in which Big Bear asked him to retrieve
the bundle.

The file contains a transcript of his meeting with museum
officials in which they pointedly ask why he arrived an hour
and fifteen minutes late, and deflect his laments about the
shortness of the meeting by reminding him of his tardiness.
The meeting is a formality; they have no intention of giving
him the bundle. They ask about his run, imply he did most
of it by car. Ask about his past, the drug and alcohol abuse,
to which he admits without hesitation.

At the end, as the museum PR man tries to shake him off
in the parking lot, Thunder mildly hopes that given how poor
the Cree are and how difficult it is to travel to New York, a
museum official might come to them to continue the
discussion. He is told that may be possible, sometimes we
have people going up there on business.

It's raining again. Scent from basil — pathetic, lead–
infused, in the window box. I like the rain — it doesn't matter
that it's dark in here, it's dark everywhere. I look out the
window, my attention caught by the movement of grey —
pigeons on the fire escape across the street.

Big Bear died in 1888. He led the River People band in the
rebellion of 1885 when the Indians and Métis fought against
the settlement of the west and were defeated by the Canadian
army. Louis Riel was hanged; Big Bear was imprisoned in the
Stoney Mountain Penitentiary in Manitoba.

In the accession file, a xeroxed newspaper photograph of
Jim Thunder shows him running down a New York street
towards the museum. The *New York Times* says he wants a
bundle which contains a two-foot-long grizzly paw. The
bundle may be two feet long. The paw, on the other hand, is
sewn to a backing of red stroud cloth and can be worn easily
around the neck. Big Bear's youngest son gave the bundle to
an anthropologist travelling for the museum. The anthro-

pologist's letter says, "The man who has the bundle came up to me one day and asked if I would take the bundle and swear to keep it well. He has many children and 'there is no place for the bundle'. I shall have to give a gift in return but his main concern is finding a safe place for the medicine."

I feel twitchy reading the file. Usually I'm alone in the room but when someone from the museum comes in I wish I were reading something else.

• • •

The best time to come here is on a Friday night, it's free and almost empty. I look at a basketry hat, the design of which represents a beaver "cut open from the mouth to near the tail, the edges of the cut spread apart, and the crown of the hat inserted into the animal. Thus the animal representation encloses the hat within it."

When you skin a deer the underside of the hide as it's pulled away is silken and veined, white and light blue. Emil hung the carcass above my bed. The flesh was maroon, almost black, and shiny. This was nearly twenty years ago.

Emil Larka. His white steps, the spill on his grey pants in the dining room of the King Eddy, his kindness; and our rift.

I slept in his parlour as he called it, a small shed attached to the cabin and used for storage. We ate the deer's liver for dinner and it was just as delicate, just as delicious, as he said it would be.

His cabin was at the far end of Lousconne Inlet at the foot of the Queen Charlotte Islands. He spent Septembers there, employed by the fishery patrol to guard the spawning salmon. Off the coast was Anthony Island, half a mile from shore but nine miles from his cabin; the inlet was long. Anthony Island was the one place on the Queen Charlottes where totem poles in any number were still standing.

It rained the first four days, and bad winds made it impossible to try on the fifth. But on the sixth day, though it was still raining, Emil took me there in his aluminum motor boat. We spent two hours, if that, on the island. Emil was either with me, or waiting for me. By then we were getting on each other's nerves.

In a letter home I described the scene: "The inlet rises straight up to forested hills, moss hangs on trees fallen down and decaying under deep growth. Feet sink down wherever they touch. Emil has shown me three cricks now, the main one and two smaller ones. The third has a waterfall. The shoreline is rocky and lined with yellow kelp."

In the letter I quote some of Emil's remarks, a side of his character I had forgotten, eclipsed by the hand on my shoulder. He compared the smell of rotting shellfish to the smell from the White House. Told me that on the Queen's visit to Kitchener in 1938, she went to the shoe factory and was presented with a pair of diamond-studded shoes worth $18,000 and made by workers paid between twelve and eighteen cents an hour. He told me that if my boyfriend ever beat me I should come to him for help. "Oh," I said, "he never would." "Well" — doubting me — "if he does."

One night I was wakened by scratching and pawing on the porch. Emil got up and I heard him moving around. In the morning he told me that a marten had been after the salmon in the pail. "I heard all that noise and thought Elizabeth was trying to get out so I thought I'd better come and help the pore girl."

His leg bothered him. We took long walks through the woods but not as long as I would have liked. "That's what you do to *me*," he said after I made some reference to holding out for something. I walked on, annoyed and discouraged.

We had met the summer before in Skedans. I had hitched a ride on a fisheries patrol boat from Queen Charlotte City to the abandoned Indian village painted sixty-two years earlier by Emily Carr. The fisheries men dropped me off and said they would be back in three days. They pointed out

Emil's cabin at the mouth of the river. I pitched my tent on the beach on the other side.

The second night it stormed, and in the morning Emil's hand beat against the door of my tent. "Young missie, young missie." He took me back to his warm cabin and fed me homemade bread. We listened to CBC radio — the old chimes they used to have before the news — and then, despite my protests, to Jack Webster's talk show from Vancouver.

Emil was tall, thin, opinionated, fastidious. He painted his front steps *white*, the woman who rented his house in Sandspit told me, her eyes wide, nervous the house wouldn't be clean enough when he got back. He shoved sticks into the stove, made coffee, seemed fit as a fiddle but wasn't. Something the matter with his stomach, he said, he wasn't usually so thin.

At Christmas he sent me a box of salmon he had caught and canned himself. In the spring, on a trip to Toronto, he took me out to dinner at the King Eddy. He wore a grey suit, and I wore a grey skirt with a sagging hem, or so I feared at the time. A waiter spilled gravy in his lap and barely apologized. Emil wiped it off with his napkin.

We wrote back and forth, and he made arrangements for my visit to Anthony Island. At the beginning of September, I was riding on a special fishery boat — this time I had my own cabin, and meals on a small table with a white tablecloth — to Lousconne Inlet. "He thinks of you as his daughter," the fishery patrol officer said.

Early one morning Emil woke me by putting his hand on my shoulder. "Come into my bed," he said, and I jerked away — "No!" — sharply. "No, Emil."

He went back into the cabin: slippers, long underwear, white hair. Over breakfast, he barely spoke. He was sixty-five and I was twenty-two.

After I left, I gave the fishery officer in Queen Charlotte

City, the one who said Emil thought of me as his daughter, ten dollars to buy him a bottle of whiskey, and I wrote him a short thank you note. But he didn't write back.

The lower sections of many of the totem poles are glassed in. If you peer down over the glass you can see dust balls, a cigarette butt, one scrunched-up piece of paper.

Anthony Island was an open window in a storm. High rocks offshore were covered with birds and seals, the waves crashed against them. We reached the village site, Ninstints, by way of a narrow channel through rocky headlands into a very small bay. The island itself was the wettest place I've ever been. Dead trees, a quarter the height of the growing ones, stood like poles, brown with no branches, and so wet they crumbled and peeled to the touch. The totems were squatter in height and feature than the ones farther north and had more antagonism and less beauty.

Cemetery

Years ago in the Arctic, mild weather descended unexpectedly. It came at night while people slept in their igloos, slept so deeply they were unaware that the pile of snow on which sleds, food, and clothes had been cached was melting. Everything slid down into the mouths of dogs, even sled runners, made as they were from strips of frozen meat. When the Inuit awakened and looked outside, everything was gone. All of them, except one woman, starved to death.

The Eskimo exhibit has been all but abandoned — no one in the museum has a specialty in the field. A section of prehistoric ivories was removed because, one museum official said, they were being "boiled" by the lights. Now they're in storage.

In the old storage rooms, objects were placed on wooden shelves and trays, costumes were stored in trunks, masks were piled on open wire shelves. Until the fifties, everything was dusted with arsenic and the rooms were pumped full of cyanide to kill powder post beetles, cigarette beetles, carpet beetles. In the summer it reached 100 degrees.

Accession file, 1902-78. Letter from museum in answer to an inquiry by a Professor Graham Rowley of Ottawa on behalf of a young Inuk he met in Igloolik who asked him about a set of garments belonging to his great-grandfather. "Sending you two sets of color photographs that show the front and back of Angakok's Coat, as well as the mittens and the hat," with one set of photos to be sent to the great-grandson, "assuring him that the garments are indeed an important part of our collection here at the museum. We are, of course, interested and amazed that the memory of the garments still exists." Letter dated June 12, 1981.

Before the Eskimo collection was moved into the new storage area, the objects were frozen for two days at a temperature of forty below zero, thawed for one day, and refrozen for two more days. That process killed the bugs which had eaten their way through baleen, skin, horn. The new storage area is a 10,000 square foot room full of white metal cabinets on wheels. Each cabinet is called a range. Turn a wheel and they move apart, creating an aisle on either side of which appear 8,500 Eskimo artifacts, all tagged with computer-generated labels and placed on acid-free paper on metal trays on metal shelves. Turn the wheel again and the ranges close so no light penetrates. The humidity remains constant at between forty and fifty percent, the temperature is 68 to 72 degrees.

Ironically, this is a Canadian-made system, built and installed by a company in Drummondville, Quebec whose technicians spent six months here in 1983.

• • •

In the distance a group of Inuit hunched over an ice hole. It was the middle of winter, they had missed the caribou and were starving. A dogteam approached, and the Inuit ran towards the newcomers to warn them away from an area of rotten ice. Then with a courtesy incredible under the circumstances, they asked the visitors if they had any extra food.

"Without hesitation," wrote the fur trader, Thierry Mallet, "we unpacked our whole outfit and laid out our complete stock on the ice." He and his guide sorted out the food, separating what they could spare from what they needed for the twenty-day return trip. They kept eighty pounds of the meat, and gave away forty. Kept 310 fish, gave away 140.

In the summer Mallet's guide returned to the same spot and learned what happened. He knew that the Inuit had planned as a last resort to travel northwest towards another lake in search of musk-oxen. The guide followed their route and after half a day found a bunch of traps, a bundle of extra caribou blankets, a small grave. After another day he began to discover bodies, one after the other, sometimes two or three together, over the space of many miles. The last was a twelve-year-old girl. She had continued on, rifle in hand, five hours more.

I walk up Broadway choosing which of a dozen outstretched hands I'll put money into. Usually only women, though one woman, Lisa, annoys me. She specifies the amount she wants and it's usually two dollars. She always makes a fuss over the baby, and is always disgruntled by the amount I give. Even in summer she wears winter clothes. Never warm enough, and where else would she put them?

Those asking for money are often the most courteous people in New York. They wish me a good day when I shake my head. When I stop, they rush to tell me that "all I'm asking for is a little help. People walk past like I'm dead."

I walk through Riverside Park, pushing the baby until he's asleep, and then sit down on a bench and read a movie review by Pauline Kael: she remembers coming to New York for the first time on a day as hot as today. She walked past a tenement stoop where a man was shouting at a sobbing eighteen-month-old child. Seeing her "stricken face" he said, "You don't like it, lady? Then how do you like this?" And poured a bottle of pink soda over the child's head.

I keep putting down the magazine to picture the twelve-year-old girl moving forward after everyone else had died.

In the reference library at 42nd Street, I fill out slips for three books: *Glimpses of the Barren Lands* and *Plain Tales of the North*, both by Thierry Mallet, and a short promotional book put out by Revillon Frères for their fur-buying customers. It gives the company's address, 670 Fifth Avenue at 53rd Street. I'll walk over, it's not far. But no real information about Mallet — simply that he was president of Revillon Frères, New York, and made regular trips north. The more I read of his writing the more curious I am, drawn to him as someone who divided his time between New York and the north. I reread his splendid *Glimpses of the Barren Lands* and, for the first time, read *Plain Tales*, published five years earlier in 1925. These are one or two page tales, all memorable, some haunting. He writes about being a French soldier in the Somme in the fall of 1916 when French and Canadian troops were fighting together. He was moving quickly down a road and passed a fallen Canadian soldier. He stopped because he heard the soldier call out for water — in Cree. Mallet knelt down beside him and put his water bottle to his lips, then he began to say slowly all the Cree words he could remember. Lake, fire, bear, moose, tent, axe, canoe. "Dozens of Cree words. Then I named in Indian all the northern places I knew from Labrador to Yukon. As soon as the Cree warrior heard my first words, he caught hold of my hands with both of his own and held on to them like a drowning man. A far away look came into his dying eyes, his features relaxed and a smile hovered on his lips."

I walk along 53rd Street towards Fifth Avenue. From the picture in the book, it should be a narrow old building, handsome, on the corner. It's there. Grey, narrow, tall, a Double day outlet now. I go inside. "No," the man behind the counter tells me. "This is 673 Fifth Avenue." "Where is 670?" I ask. He doesn't know. I cross the street. St. Thomas Church is on one corner, a new skyscraper is on the other, a Benetton store at ground level. This must be it. Gone.

Thierry Mallet wrote about an Indian who travelled from the far north to Montreal, never having seen a car or electric light or railway. Nothing surprised him. "In Montreal he seemed to fight shy of the streets and preferred to remain in the lobby of the small hotel where a room had been reserved for him. He sat there all day, looking through the window." Only one thing astonished him: that so many people passed each other and never stopped to speak, never acknowledged each other in any way.

In Yellowknife an Inuit woman told me about coming to New York. After a day her face ached because she smiled at everyone she passed.

• • •

In 1919, Robert Flaherty the American film maker was trudging the streets of New York with a burned partial print of his first film under his arm (he had dropped his cigarette on the film, but wasn't sorry; he knew it wasn't any good). He wanted to make a second one and was looking for a backer. He found Thierry Mallet. Mallet convinced Revillon Frères to put up the money for *Nanook of the North*.

Flaherty made the film on the east coast of Hudson Bay. According to his wife's account, the Inuit of Port Harrison did everything for him. They chiseled through six feet of ice to get water for washing his film and kept the hole open all winter. They combed the coastline for driftwood to make a drying reel. They cleaned and repaired his cameras, and devised a method for printing film by the light of the low arctic sun. Sometimes the film shattered like glass from the cold, so Nanook carried it next to his skin, along with the camera, and called them his "babies."

In the movie Nanook visits the fur trader's post and listens to a gramophone. Playfully, he bites the disc (it might be Harry Lauder's "Stop Your Ticklin' Jock," or Caruso, or Al Jolson and the Jazz King Orchestra). He catches fish and kills them with his teeth, harpoons a walrus whose mate then struggles to pull it free, takes a live white fox from a trap and ties it, still alive, to his sled. He licks his ivory snowknife to glaze the surface of the blade, then cuts blocks of snow for an igloo. He fashions an ice window, and erects beside it a fin-like slab of snow to reflect more light inside.

The film was first shown in 1922. Two years later Nanook starved to death. In 1932, Flaherty's wife was in Berlin and bought an Eskimo pie in the Tiergarten. "It was called a 'Nanuk'," she wrote, "and Nanook's face smiled up at me from the wrapper."

Dzonokwa

Across the street a woman with large gold earrings leans out a second floor window into the rain. Glint and weight of gold. Dark skin. Her elbows rest on a pillow.

I know her. Lily. She writes poetry in the café on the corner and sometimes I join her for coffee. She asks me what I'm writing and I mention self-deprecation — I want to pursue the roots of self-deprecation in Canadian mythology yet feel the need to write about New York, and remain confused by the two directions.

She says, "But isn't it there? You are to Canadian mythology as Canada is to New York."

Manhattan is the back of a turtle. According to the Lenape Indians the world began when a turtle rose up from the ocean and a tree grew on its back. From the tree's roots sprang the first man, and from the branch as it bent down to touch the ground — the first woman.

Canada's mythology is the mythology of not having one, of being inarticulate about our past. Like a deep blush, this can be eloquent in itself.

New York is the backdrop against which Canada comes clear as self-conscious, self-defeating, and, in certain ways, full of charm. The most dominant Canadian myth, the one we tell ourselves over and over again, is that we aren't much good. In this myth New York is the escape, the opposite polarity.

On Saturday night at Fat Tuesday's, a small jazz club, Cassandra Wilson sings six feet away. I take my cue from Alec — clapping with enthusiasm when he does, agreeing that the piano player is better than Cassandra although she is "very good." Halfway through, I lift my cold drink as I look, nod, smile at Alec, and stick myself in the nose with my straw.

This apartment has moonlight and lamplight. It always edges towards being and back to not-being. A certain hesitation, approach and retreat, living by gradation, which reminds me of the lives of women, and of Canadians.

Curious, that a country founded on trapping puts itself down. When you put down an animal, you kill it.

In the garbage bin this morning — surprisingly slender, attractive — but I slammed the lid shut, stamped my foot twice in horror. RAT.

How did animals lose their power of speech? How do we become tongue-tied?

How did it happen that conversation between animals and humans ceased?

Generations ago, Inuit children were dressed in jackets made from the skin of young deer and caps made from the heads; fawn ears poked up on either side of small human ears.

The children listened to their animal selves — those inarticulate, background figures we are as children.

Pitseolak remembered things from before he was able to walk. He remembered looking into caribou eyes, "they were so close": he was lying on the ground as his mother waved her parka to direct the caribou towards the hunters. He remembered being born. He went through a crevice in the ice (his mother's bones) and when he opened his eyes he saw two little cliffs (her thighs) and something blue. After he was born, he never cried. He was too busy looking around.

In a Brazilian myth, the blood of a dismembered child becomes the means by which birds acquire coloured plumage. The process of seeking some sort of comfort in a violent and tragic ending, of twisting the story so that it becomes something else, seems to be typical of myths. Many myths dwell on the loss of children. Dzonokwa myths, for instance, are about the great fear of losing your children, and the greater fear of losing your childhood — entering the dark and inarticulate woods of puberty.

The Dzonokwa mask is the bottommost one in a wall case of Kwakiutl artifacts. Black face, one thick furry eyebrow extended over both sunken eyes, moustache, small chin beard, red and hollow cheeks, red protruding lips. The mouth is open in a permanent stammer, the face contorted by its effort to speak.

One day in the woods, a princess met "a big stout woman" who stammered because she had a speech impediment. The big woman — a Dzonokwa — admired the princess's plucked eyebrows and promised to make her a gift of magical garments if she would show her how to be beautiful. The princess took her back to her village where a barber — a warrior in disguise — killed her with hammer and chisel.

At puberty, girls wear the same magical garments of goat's hair that Dzonokwa gave the princess.

Sunken-eyed, hollow-cheeked, open-mouthed, trimmed

with fur. Woman gone wrong. Endowed with breasts, beard, and moustache, Dzonokwa dwells deep in the woods, alone in her sexual ambiguity, ambiguous in her loneliness, and hungry. She carries off children in a bag over her shoulder.

In Dzonokwa, puberty is writ large — the hesitance, the shame, the unhappiness. At puberty we become more animal-like even as we become less so, sprouting hair and hesitance even as we lose an animal's unself-consciousness. In Indian cultures boys used to set off, and through dreams and visions commune with the animals who would be their protectors. Afterwards they returned to the villages, strengthened and prepared for the future. What comes of not making the voyage, of entering the edge of animal being but not pushing forward? One's life is defined by that — by remaining stuck, trapped, on the edge; border of fur; black border of being.

The myths of Dzonokwa, wild woman of the woods, crea-ture of cavities associated with vaginal coming of age, origi-nated on the northwest coast in Knight Inlet, the deepest fjord in Kwakiutl territory. She was always killed by people who promised to make her better looking.

Emily Carr painted Dzonokwa as she found her, surround-ed by cats in an abandoned village. By then she had come upon her at least three times on totem poles in different vil-lages, and each time she was less menacing. On the final occa-sion the features on the pole seemed completely feminine.

Emily — isolated, inarticulate. "I expect I shall only be able to sit like a bell without a tongue and just make a note if someone kicks me." She preferred letters to conversation. "That beastliness, self-consciousness, is left out ... getting rattled and mislaying words."

Inuit mythology has a being similar to Dzonokwa. Kalopaling wears a jacket with an enormous hood. He cannot talk, can only cry, Be, be! Be, be! He kidnaps children — stealing back his talkative childhood?

After puberty, words escaped me. I sat at the dining room

table and tried to write essays for school, appalled that words could be so elusive.

• • •

Red/pink, scab off my lip, colour of hibiscus. In Kwakiutl mythology, Scab marries a Dzonokwa who stammers, then marries the daughter of the sun and falls off when he rides on her back up to the sky. Proper fate of a scab, to fall off.

Cold sore scab — New York City labret. The absence of talk blossoms, ugly/decorative, hibiscus on my lip.

"Your stress comes out in your lips," says Alec. That tense area between saying nothing and saying something badly. Canadian: you know it's there but you can't put your finger on it. Inarticulate: you know the words are there, you can sense their shape and meaning, but they escape you.

At Lily's reading, the line, "I found it difficult to talk," came out at me.

My disquiet afterwards. Because she introduced me to none of her friends? Because when I went to tell her how much I liked her reading I hugged her and tears came to my eyes, more tears, another hug, but more tears, so that she asked, are you all right? Her question made sense and my tears none at all. I left quickly, undetained by her.

To come home and write about being inarticulate in this city of talk.

Lily and I have a Canadian/American friendship. I feel a certain dread whenever she calls. What does she want this time? How is she going to take advantage of me this time? And I feel inferior. The calls go on for a long time and I rarely understand a word she says. I hear her say things I want to remember but by the time she hangs up I've forgotten. She talks the language of an advanced writer who thinks about writing in a very sophisticated way.

For instance, there was the conversation we had in the Cuban restaurant. Here I was able to watch her face, command her full attention, and still I didn't understand. She said, "What matters most to me in writing is composition." I asked her if she meant the structure of the piece. "I mean," she said, "that the world speaks through language."

She was wearing green, and a necklace that was green and brown and set off her black hair. The windows next to our table were full of reflections which distracted me.

I understood one piece of advice: "Imagine that you're looking outside and you see a woman disappearing into the snow. Now write that scene and make yourself disappear from it. For instance," she said, "don't impute motives."

There was something very Canadian about her American advice. Don't draw attention to yourself, she was saying, and what is more Canadian than that? What, after all, did the writer Robert Fulford, Glenn Gould's childhood friend, say about Gould's mother? He said, "She didn't like Glenn to have opinions that were too confident. Too showing off. She was a real old-fashioned Canadian in that way. Don't come out of hiding too much, and never give an opinion that isn't well considered, and probably don't give it at all."

Canadians start out drawing attention to themselves by drawing too little attention to themselves — the dilemma of the shy — and move on to drawing attention to themselves directly, the way Americans do, and end up, some of them, drawing less attention to themselves than to everything around them. This was the whole thrust of Glenn Gould's life, and Borduas's life, and Emily Carr's. They struggled to lose themselves in something larger. They took the old Canadian hangup and turned it into a virtue. It takes an American, Lily, to make me realize this.

• • •

A woman knew where snow had fallen and went to see if any of those spots bore traces of the event. She pulled on the clothesline — snow had turned the dark rope a lighter blue. She fingered the rope and remembered the snow.

She went out onto the fire escape. The black paint was less glossy where snow had sat, and she now sat, remembering. She examined the hard white roof of the car, scratched and dull from various winters. On television they showed pictures of a blizzard to remind people of what snow was.

She got northern books out of the library. In one she read about a Cree woman whose husband was blind. "But I did not feel sorry for him," the woman said, "in that he still saw birds. He talked about them clearly, as if he had been out walking among them that morning. So, you see, it was not as if he saw nothing in his eyes. He often had summer birds in them . . . even during winter."

It was 100 degrees. She put down her book and went outside. She walked slowly and with a handkerchief, the handkerchief loose and damp, a soft white cane tapping her face and neck.

Wicker, she found, was cooler than wood. Tiles were cooler than wicker. Mirrors cooler still.

She looked in the mirror and saw the cool bones of her face. It was quiet except for the drone of the refrigerator. She listened and remembered a story: a man from the highlands of Guatemala carried a refrigerator on his back all the way to the border of Mexico. He entered a refugee camp, set down the refrigerator, set up his hammock and stretched out. His was the only refrigerator in the camp. When customers came, he called to his daughter who came out and sold them cold sodas.

The woman fell asleep thinking about the girl reaching into the refrigerator. In the morning she got up early and went outside and saw Cold dying in the street: a refrigerator without a door, the inside disembowelled, insulation the colour of sand. She came back inside and dipped her hands in icy water and let Cold chew on the fleshy tips of her fingers.

I walk through the dim apartment to the fluorescent light over the sink and make coffee, washing out the small blue enamel pan with a blue sponge — quiet movements, preparatory to pleasure. Cream. Sugar.

I drink it standing by the round wooden table, and look towards the far end of the apartment, my desk, the windows tall and narrow, covered with wrought-iron gates and penetrated by low-level light.

I smell Yellowknife — clearly, in whiffs. The sweet smell of that terrific coldness, eyelashes freezing shut as I walked my dog after dark, past houses, woods, more houses, up to the slight hill just below Father Fumoleau's house, just before the final rise which dipped down into Rainbow Valley — treaty land. I turned right, followed the road to the other side of the island, houses set high — and the air sweet somehow, our breath freezing on fur — Stan's muzzle, the edge of my parka hood. Sometimes we walked on Great Slave Lake itself following the tracks of ski planes and skidoos. And always that sweet air — part woodsmoke, part animal, part human, and many things that weren't any of those.

I read Boas again — his steady progression through the particulars of Inuit life: a strip of whalebone sharpened at either end is rolled up and held with sinew, then buried in a piece of meat and swallowed by the pestering wolf; the sinews dissolve, the whalebone uncoils.

Such beautiful light over my desk — whalebone light inside the dark stomach of this apartment.

• • •

The day the weather broke, her lip split. Cold came out of that crack, that pout of longing.

There was a time — cool in the morning, hot at midday, cool in the evening — when hot and cold talked to each other. When words came alive and, as an old Inuit song says, "what people wanted to happen could happen."

The Fifth Remove

On the weathered door
wood-hairs leave shadow-lines on the
hot wood.

MARGARET AVISON
SKETCH: *A childhood place*

Canada

In late August we drive to Canada and spend five days at my family's cabin on a semi-wilderness lake. My parents are here, my brother, my sister-in-law, my nephew. The cabin has no electricity or plumbing and we cook on a woodstove. It's dark because my parents refuse to cut down any trees.

On a walk through the woods my brother picks wintergreen. He crushes it between his fingers and holds it under my nose: "Guess what it is," he says. I can't. He picks wild thyme (patches of it in purple blossom) and crushes it between his fingers: "Guess." And I do.

Doll's eyes and wild raspberries grow along the road, walking fern and cardinal flowers grow in the woods. My brother identifies them.

After dark we go out in the canoe and hear two loons, their echo; a hawk, its baby cry; many beaver. Bats skim the surface of the water. The night is clear and still with a slightly more than half moon. At nine thirty the wind comes up and it's cooler.

One afternoon my sister-in-law explains a game that she played as a girl. Two teams, each with a captain, hide from the other; team members communicate with one another by passwords. Beaver might mean stay still. Orange — come slowly. Grapefruit — go to the right. Her clues are fur and citrus. Why do they come to mind? Why those words?

And then we go out in the canoe and peel oranges as we watch for beaver, and the image I've been carrying in my head for years — explorers called furs the fruit of their labours — comes alive.

In what little pre-breakfast light there is, my mother does tai-chi at the foot of the cedar. Her face is old, older than I've ever seen it, soft and drawn and without colour.

In the evening, standing beside the pale forms of three overturned canoes while we look at the moon and rain falls lightly, she tells me why she is so tired. Last winter she fell on the ice and her neck still hurts; sleep is difficult. She moves much more carefully and for the first time I think of her as fragile. I am angry that she never told me about her fall, and I feel a new responsibility. I shouldn't be so far away.

She shows me slides of her drawings of arctic bones on a velvety black background, made to look, she says, like jewels displayed on velvet. Her preoccupations are never very different from what they've always been, and never very different from mine. Years ago she was painting jewels against a black background to give the idea of menace and mourning. And now she is mourning for the natural world.

At midnight our hair is damp from swimming.

My sister-in-law dreams that a man in a truck is chasing her (she is wearing my mother's dress, and is taller). She reaches her block (the archway of trees we walked under yesterday) and the man still pursues her. She knows she is all right, even though she doesn't move when she runs, because she has rice in her pocket. She throws some rice into the air and the leg of a grizzly bear appears. More rice and the second leg. She needs enough time to throw all the rice so that the grizzly will appear completely and protect her. As the man closes in, and before the grizzly has more than two legs, she wakes up.

I work her dream into a story about a white bear going south. In the heat a bear sheds more and more of its hair, and wherever a hair falls snow springs up. The bear's route becomes a cool pathway and many animals follow it south. Years go by, the animals tire of the heat and decide to return home, but by then none of the path remains; animals coming south have licked at it until it is all gone.

The bear has some rice in his pocket. He throws the rice and the snowy left side of the route springs back into place. He throws more rice and the right side appears. The animals walk north. When they get hungry they fill a pot with snow from the pathway and melt it into rice soup. The soup is very nourishing. It's all they need.

When I began writing about Canadians in New York, I thought of them as talismans. Their invisible presence made me feel safer and more alive.

Before we begin the drive back, Alec says, "Look at this. You'll want to remember this in New York."

"What do you like most?" I ask him. "The quiet, first of all," he answers. "The size of the trees, the animals, the canoes."

Those images — the quiet, and the size of the trees — are the ones that stay with me as we drive into New York.

The Sixth Remove

Children hear a soft and gentle voice, almost like that of a woman. It comes to them in a mysterious way, but so gently that they are not afraid; they only hear that some danger is threatening. And the children mention it as it were casually when they come home . . .

NAJAGNEQ
Alaska, 1924

Seductions

Sometimes I realize I may never go back. About a year ago I was standing on a corner waiting for the light to turn, and in a mood of sick alarm started to count: one year in Salem, two years in Brooklyn, one year in Manhattan. We came intending to stay two years; we still have no plans to leave.

My father's assumption crossed my mind: my daughter has married an American and that's where she will stay. My husband crossed my mind: his willingness to leave disguising a strong desire to stay. My children know nothing of Canada.

Captivity tales are about early settlers carried off by Indians. It's a genre, one of the oldest of American literary forms. Now I write captivity tales-in-reverse. Rather than settlers carried off by Indians, Eskimos stranded in New York. Fears have changed. A fear of the wilderness has been replaced by a fear of cities.

In the original captivity tales, people were removed from "civilization" and carried farther and farther — from one remove to the next — into Indian territory. With some exceptions, they treated captivity as a nightmare with no bearing on their real lives; once released, they wrote long narratives praising God. The more removed from Canada the more appalled I feel, yet each remove takes me farther, perhaps, into some kind of Indian territory, which is exactly where I want to be.

In 1755, when she was twelve years old, Mary Jemison and her family were captured by the French and the Indians. They spent two full days walking without food or water, and then an Indian took off Mary's shoes and stockings, put moccasins on her feet, and led her away from the others into the bush. Later, the Indians "made me to understand" that they wouldn't have killed her family had the whites not pursued them. That night she watched them scrape the scalps of her mother, father, two brothers, and sister. "My mother's hair was red, and I could easily distinguish my father's and the children's from each other."

Two Seneca women adopted her. Their brother had been killed and Mary was his replacement: "a prisoner or an enemy's scalp, to supply their loss." She spent four summers and four winters living at first with the two women and then with her Indian husband, and she was happy. She paints an almost frieze-like portrait of their existence. "Notwithstanding the Indian women have all the fuel and bread to procure, and the cooking to perform, their task is probably not harder than that of white women, who have those articles provided for them; and their cares certainly are not half as numerous, nor as great. In the summer season we planted, tended and harvested our corn, and generally had all our children with us; but had no master to oversee or drive us, so that we could work as leisurely as we pleased."

At the end of four years, she had the chance to go free. The king offered a bounty for every prisoner taken in the war, and her response was to hide. She hid first from a Dutch trader who wanted to take her to the military post at Niagara and collect the bounty, and later from an Indian who wanted to do the same.

When James Seaver took down her account of her life, she was eighty years old, with light blue eyes and grey hair tied behind in a knot. "She speaks English plainly and distinctly, with a little of the Irish emphasis, walks with a quick step without a staff and could yet cross a stream on a log or pole as steadily as any other person." She was dressed in the Indian fashion, in a shirt, short gown, petticoat, stockings, moccasins, blanket, and bonnet.

• • •

It's hard to remember Canada. Not hard to remember. Hard to concentrate on the memory.

My mother pulled lichen-covered birchbark off the dead

tree that fell in the night, and gave me three pieces. I have them on my desk.

Let Canada come here.

• • •

When Minik went back north, it didn't work out. Nor did it work out for Hannah. She went back with Hall, and then returned south with him. After he died, she could have gone home but chose to stay here.

I sit in the old rocking chair from Renfrew and listen to Stan Getz; tired, and Stan so restful, beautiful. Ben climbs into my lap. Maybe he'll remember this, jazz in a soft lap in New York City.

It isn't relaxing or expansive, this business of being Canadian, at least not the way I'm living it: uncertain about whether to go back and when, distrusting my desire to return even while I believe in it, thinking about little else.

I should be making dinner, but sit here listening to music and thinking of Theresa upstairs, of our friendship, our system of collective cooking and childcare which reminds me of the life of pioneers. We cook one night, they cook the next, and we share the food. They are so scrupulous about not taking advantage, so deeply generous. We have a good life here, and still I want to uproot us. I want Alec to quit his job. I want to go home.

You could say that missing Canada is a product of fear, an incapacity to be in New York rather than a product of love of country. It's an escape both from the reality of here and the reality of there.

You could say that, and not be wrong.

Which tune is this? "Thanks for the Memory" (Rainger-Robin). Recorded in New York City, December 12th, 1952.

• • •

Minik arrived back in the Arctic wearing clothes suitable

for New York: short socks and everyday shoes, writes his biographer. On one of his first hunting trips, he went inland for several days, found no caribou, came back weak and hungry, and in English — which no one could understand — said, "I am so miserable and useless that I didn't even see one caribou." Although he learned how to hunt and hunt well, he remained "listless and sullen." He married a woman who was cross-eyed and lazy, and he left her.

He returned to New York seven years later on September 21st, 1916. He took a room at the McAlpin Hotel, "appeared briefly in a Vaudeville routine dressed up in Eskimo garb," travelled a year later to the lumber town of Pittsburgh, New Hampshire. Worked for fifty cents a day. Built himself a tiny shack "up across from the little cemetery where the unclaimed river drivers were buried," near the spot where he too would be buried, before long.

Kudlago almost made it home. He had been brought to the United States in 1859 by the whaling captain, Sidney Budington. A year later he was sailing north as Charles Hall's first interpreter. He died at sea. "His last words were, 'Teik-ko se-ko? Teik-ko se-ko?' Do you see ice? Do you see ice?"

Kudlago's wife met the ship. "As she looked at us," writes Hall, "and then at the chest where Kudlago had kept his things, the tears flowed faster and faster . . . her grief could hardly be controlled when the treasures Kudlago had gathered in the States for her and his little girl were exhibited. A pretty red dress, a necktie, mittens, a belt. She sat herself down upon the chest, and pensively bent her head in deep, unfeigned sorrow; then, after a time, she left the cabin with her son."

In Groton, Connecticut, the Starr Cemetery has the following headstones:

> *Cudlargo [sic], died July 1, 1860, age 35.*
> *Oosee, George, died July 1, 1867, age 28.*

Tukiltkitar, died Feb. 28, 1863, age 18 months.
Silvia G.E., adopted daughter of Joe and
   Hannah, died Mar. 18, 1875.
Eberbing, Hannah, wife of Joseph, died Dec. 31,
   1876, age 38.

After we looked at the tablets on the ground, and at
Hannah's tombstone, we drove on and saw a friend whose
depression was so deep that she couldn't distinguish between
her sadness and the heat outside. We found a fan covered
with dust in one corner, and we opened the windows. I swept
the floor and found a scrap of paper with the words, "It's
scary to see how much I've deteriorated."

• • •

Now I think about the effects of living for two years in a
tube of darkness with light at one end. It reminds me of a
movie theatre. The perfect darkness for a movie theatre.
   My daughter and I are awash in old musicals — a New York
life within New York. When we walk down Broadway, she
says, "Tell me *The Pirate*." I tell her the plot of the movie and
even when it seems hopelessly confusing — Manuela admires
Macoco the famous pirate and so Serafin pretends to be
Macoco even though Don Pedro, the man she's engaged to,
is the real Macoco — she listens. She never says I don't
understand. She just says, "Tell me. Tell me."
   I listen with the same attention to talk about Canada. The
sound of the words is enough. We don't have to understand
or agree, we just want to hear the names spoken out loud.
   Last night I dreamt that I was sitting in a sloping chair on
a flat roof three feet from the edge. Directly below — a
quarter of a mile down — was the ocean. I kept reassuring
myself that I couldn't fall off, I was three feet away after all,
but I felt myself slipping in the weirdly constructed chair. I
also dreamt that Ginger Rogers finally confessed that she and

Fred Astaire had made love twice. Fred had written some verses about it which ended with another weird construction: a combination of awfully and enticing — awticing.

This room, hour, light — a pool of light over the kitchen table, the sound of water running upstairs, and footsteps, clear but faint. This quiet time early in the morning while the children sleep — this secret — secret time. I even forsake boasting about how early I get up so that people won't be able to picture me here. I want to picture them. I want to be alone and awake while others sleep.

I feel braver in the early hours. A circle of light, a cup of coffee, a notepad. I feel less out of touch, no doubt because everything I'm out of touch with is out of sight.

On the table: a child's pair of sunglasses, sugar bowl, teapot, empty juice bottle, half a lemon, a bottle of glue, a yogurt container full of crayons, a newspaper. I pick it up and read a story about "The Tourist Murder." A photo in the left hand corner shows the tourist's nine-year-old sister, and her quote runs across the front page: My Brother Is a Hero But He's Not Coming Back.

A bullet sits on top of the chest of drawers. It looks like a dark grey mushroom, smeared on one side. It went through the back door of our car, ploughed through several bags of old magazines in the back seat and came to rest on the November 15th, 1952 issue of *The Nation*. Alec's father kept every back issue, and after he died we put them in bags and brought them to New York to add to the *Nation*'s archives. The bullet blasted a hole clean through fifty copies, then shredded the last ten before coming to a halt.

We weren't in the car. It was parked one block over at 104th and Amsterdam. We show people the hole in the door and they're always impressed.

Rain now — tires, wet sounds, the window open. We're at ground level and New Yorkers are loud. They pass by the window and no matter what they're talking about it sounds like a fight.

New York habits I've picked up: when someone phones and asks me how I am, I no longer say so-so, or not too bad. I say good. (It's not that Americans are necessarily happier than Canadians, but they won't admit to sadness.)

I talk more.

I apologize less.

I kill cockroaches with my fist.

The people who ask for money in the street are no longer as polite, and nor am I.

Fred Astaire arrives in Grand Central Station. He takes a taxi to Times Square, circles around bewildered by everything he doesn't recognize, then dances as he gets a shoeshine. This is already the fifties — one of his later movies — and he's playing a song-and-dance man who makes a comeback.

A younger Fred Astaire sings with Ginger Rogers ("We should be like a couple of hot tomatoes/But you're as cold as yesterday's mashed potatoes"), woos Joan Leslie as she takes pictures in a nightclub, and smash-dances every glass in the place.

We watch each musical at least twice, and only on the weekends.

Paradox: I feel more connected to New York when I watch this earlier New York which didn't even exist. More connected to myself when I perch above me and watch. More connected to Canada when I'm not there.

My daughter and I watch Ruby Keeler in *Forty-Second Street*. I tell her that Ruby was born in Canada and moved to New York when she was four years old. Her father sold ice. In *Forty-Second Street* she gets thrown out of her boarding house for helping a man who has been beaten up, goes to his place to sleep because she doesn't have money for a hotel, and observes with watchful deer-like eyes as he turns the lights low. She's different from Deanna Durbin. Sochi and I watch Deanna Durbin too. She appears with Judy Garland in a short called *Every Sunday* and is wholesome, rather wooden, very pleasant: a Canadian to Judy's electrifying American. Deanna is as clean and "frankly unspoiled" as Ruby but without the uncalculating sexuality that appeals to obnoxious men. Al Jolson wooed Ruby with two dozen roses the first night, a cameo toilet set the second night, a lynx fur coat the third night, and himself the fourth night.

We don't watch Norma Shearer but I read about her. Her father was a failed Montreal businessman who told her that "life is filled with hanging wires. You have to avoid jangling the wires if you want to reach the exit." F. Scott Fitzgerald wrote a story about Norma — one crackup writing about another. Her father and sister were mentally ill, and friends said of Norma that "there was always something funny back there."

The Canadian who truly got lost in the movies was Marie Prevost. She became a leading star in the twenties only to fade out when the talkies arrived; her voice was not "dynaphonic." She gained weight, became an alcoholic, went on a crash diet, then stopped eating altogether. In 1937, at the age of thirty-eight, her body was found in her Hollywood apartment. She had been dead for two days, and her dachshund had eaten some of her flesh.

I like my Canadians dead, it seems.

I've seen two Canadian T-shirts in three days. One said Montreal. The other, Toronto. My reaction was curiosity spiked with distaste. Who are these interlopers, I wondered, these ordinary joes wearing Canada on their chests? Don't they know Canada belongs to me?

When I think about what I miss, I have exact thoughts: medicare, decent schools, empty space, small towns. I miss hearing *okeedokee* on the phone.

When I think about going back, my thoughts are inexact,

just as they become inexact when I bump into Canadians in the street. Why aren't you wonderful, I think; I'm wonderful. A wonderful Canadian in awful New York. Am I not so wonderful then? And I turn away, bad-tempered.

It's not that one place spoils the other, but that it becomes easier to hold a place in your mind if you're living somewhere else, and it becomes more important to hold the place in your mind than to be there.

• • •

A morning of writing letters. Then I pick up Elena Poniatowska's *Dear Diego*, a book of fictional letters, all unanswered. How beautifully they're written, how simple and full of emotion. From Quiela, the woman Diego Rivera lived with in Paris for ten years. They had a son, the son died, Diego went back to Mexico. Quiela wrote to him and he never answered.

How we wait! How women wait. Waiting for Canada. Waiting for light. Waiting for life to fill up and make sense. Waiting for words to arrive.

I told Alec as we were driving from Boston back to New York that it's the disloyalty that bothers me most. New England is more beautiful than anywhere I've been in Canada, I could be happy there, except for the nagging inescapable feeling that I'd sold out.

"You mean you feel you ought to be in Canada struggling to make the country better, fighting for things?"

"No. I don't mean that. You know I don't struggle for things. No, it's simpler than that, so simple it's complicated. I can't face myself as an American."

Quiela keeps reminding Diego of their past together, making it real to him and to herself. Somehow the letters aren't full of self-pity. They're so intense, so felt, they aren't even pathetic.

Hers is unrequited love, and mine could be requited. All I

have to do is move back. In the first letters she complains very
little. She tries not to be a burden; to remind him that she is
worth having. She uses the phrase *le mal du pays*, the
homesickness Diego had for Mexico. "You would turn your
eyes towards that pale sun and remember another one, and
deep down you already wanted to leave."

And so Diego was loyal by being disloyal.

• • •

In late summer we walk along Duke Ellington Boulevard
to Central Park. The park is lush and dusty and used. Muddy
pondwater, spent roses, soft dogshit. The air is soupy with
the past and present. Layer upon layer of urban life bubbles
over in a yeastiness that is sour and pungent and captivating.
A tall white heron stands on a dead log, then shifts — flying
low — to a bed of weeds.

The nature of love, I think to myself. My emotional tie to
Canada is less the edgy one between husband and wife than
the deeper, less describable one with a child: an all-
enveloping and loaded combination of censure and accept-
ance. Would I feel this way if I hadn't lived in New York?

We walk over New Brunswick sandstone, quarried by
Acadians and brought here by sloop and schooner to be
made into Central Park bridges, and up a hill planted with
roses. In this still wild, still beautiful park the air is heavy with
scent.

I loved New York the first time I came. The furs on Fifth
Avenue, the fresh cut flowers. It was a relief to be somewhere
so different. I watched people stream past Grand Central
Station early in the morning with sweet rolls and coffee-to-go.
The romance of people with a lot on their minds.

We picnic in the sun, then come home in the late afternoon
to all the qualities of darkness: a vase of dark red flowers in
the long throat of the apartment — velvet petals — animal
darkness — quiet. It could be five in the morning. Any time

of day here is five in the morning. I sit next to the flowers and listen to the hum of the refrigerator, murmur of northern stories.

In 1894, snow fell on the Eskimos in Dr. Frederick Cook's back yard on West 55th Street, and while it lasted they were exuberant. They were living in a tent, two boys about thirteen years old. They accompanied Cook as he strolled down the street with two northern dogs. According to the *New York Times*, large crowds of boys used to follow them. Neighbours said that although they knew almost no English, they could "cuss like troopers."

A year earlier, Cook — Peary's future rival for the North Pole — had appeared at Huber's Dime Museum on 14th Street with "an Eskimo outfit." He set up an Eskimo camp on the main stage and gave lectures nine times a day for four weeks. John Henderson, the owner of the Dime Museum, told the *Times* that "The weather was pretty warm for it was in May that he appeared with the show and I noticed that the Eskimos suffered acutely. Besides the Eskimos were half a dozen dogs with the exhibition and these Dr. Cook put through some kind of performance. The dogs seemed to suffer from the heat about as much as the Eskimos."

One of the Eskimos died. They had been brought to the Chicago World's Fair in 1892, abandoned by their promoter, and picked up by Dr. Cook "out of the goodness of his heart."

Plums

Along Broadway (once an Indian trail) the air has the pink pearliness, unclear and dusty, of a day that starts hot and gets hotter. Plum trees used to grow wild and in September the island was blue with fruit. A hundred springs used to water the woods and meadow; they still run beneath the pavement.

In the library I read microfilm, my hands in the moonlight and shadow of words. It could be midnight, with cars — their headlights on — passing by outside. The effect is leafy.

Writing leaves, creating shade. Inuktitut doesn't have words for shades of blue. Just a dark blue, or light blue, or a kind of blue. But not turquoise, teal, peacock blue. Which is curious since snow is really blue not white, and they have dozens of words for snow.

Manhattan used to be tundra. Mastodons and mammoths used to roam the continental shelf; their teeth have been dredged up and taken from the banks of a now submerged portion of the Hudson River. After the glacier retreated, plants grew back in four stages: tundra, subarctic forest, coniferous forest, deciduous.

On the wall behind me are my mother's arctic paintings. She has written in her careful hand "Arctic lichen, clodonia gracilis" beneath mildew-white lichen painted on handmade paper. This soil isn't so foreign after all. Tundra reindeer moss still grows among the peaks of the Hudson Highlands.

Just for the pleasure of it, I make a list of all the trees found in the Hudson Valley: red oak, pin oak, black oak, rock chestnut, swamp hickory, small-fruited hickory, mountain laurel, hackberry, white ash, red pine, red cedar, sweet gum, tamarack, sycamore, white elm, flowering dogwood, mountain magnolia, black willow, sassafras, red mulberry, tulip tree, red maple, sugar maple, witch hazel and river birch; and the perfume which comes off the page is lusher than a Canadian woods and fresher than anything tropical.

The Hudson River flows from north to south through the Canadian Shield, the Folded Appalachians, the Hudson Highlands, the New England Upland, and the New Jersey Lowland. Its valley "serves as a long, finger-like extension of the south": plants normally found in Virginia grow here, and certain southern animals live year round, while in the highlands Canadian warblers make their nests. Geographers call the valley a tension zone — a meeting ground between north and south — a fluid sort of place, and one that should suit me and, I suppose if I let it, it would.

The Algonquins were the first to settle the valley. They came seeking a river that flowed two ways and found it in the tidal Hudson. When the tide comes in the river flows upstream. It offers two directions almost simultaneously: leaving home and going home, which seems to be what I do continually in my mind.

The Seventh Remove

The real secret of the ruby slippers is not that 'there's no place like home' but, rather, that there is no longer any such place as home — except, of course, for the homes we make, or the homes that are made for us, in Oz. Which is anywhere — and everywhere — except the place from which we began.

SALMAN RUSHDIE

Houdini

Snow reasserts itself under any tan. I walk past brown summer faces and see snow falling, skin going white like the ground.

September. We moved two years ago into this light, a different tone each month. Silver in September, blonde in October, white in November.

It's four in the afternoon. In the middle of the apartment a light is on. And here beside the window — pretty light, pale, wallflower light. Reminiscent of no time of day I'm familiar with: too light for dawn, too unchanging for dusk, not light enough for day — some internal light. Onion inside its skin. At five I lower the shades. We have eleven lights in two rooms: Inuvik without the solitude.

On September 27th I wake up to the smell of heat — that singed smell of comfort from radiators unused all summer — and the slow appearance of light from six to seven. A warm screen, soft emergence of shapes, everything quiet, everyone asleep.

Flickering images of Nanook, flickering images of Marie Prevost: almost the same period — silent movies — and the same Canadian fate: starvation. One in Hollywood, the other in the Arctic.

The temperature has dropped, the air turned dry. All the summer humidity has suddenly gone.

We drive into the country and walk through fields. The sound of crickets is continuous. A few leaves have turned, but only a few. Blackberries ripen.

For a few hours we walk away from New York.

Houdini used to live eight blocks away on 113th Street. He had a four-storey house with twenty-six rooms, several of which were filled with his 5,200 books on magic. He kept his crates of tricks, locks, leg irons and chains in his basement, and there he perfected his feats of escape.

Emily Carr escaped after a week. Linda Bouchard has gone to Montreal. Teresa Stratas fled to India. In an interview she said, "Even my books were not helping me escape from feeling trapped." I think of her mink coats stored in a vault, the jewelry she never wears, the parties she never attends, the performances she cancels "because terror makes her literally sick," the ones she forces herself to give in order to be somebody else for a few hours. A fearless panicked woman. After her telecast performance of *Pagliacci*, a blind boy appeared at her door with a flower.

I find F. Scott Fitzgerald's story "Crazy Sunday" about the afternoon he spent with Norma Shearer and Irving Thalberg. He calls her Stella — this Canadian girl with a cast in her left eye, too-heavy thighs, and a washed-up father. He describes her "fresh boyish face, with the tired eyelid that always drooped a little over one eye . . . a radiant, faltering smile." In the story, he makes a fool of himself telling a too-long drunken joke and only Stella stands by him.

I read Sir Charles G. D. Roberts's story about a young polar bear, captured after its mother was shot by sealers, and sold to a zoo where it was "ceaselessly irritated . . . sullenly swaying and swinging his head all day." In a heavy storm which "to his heart was the summons of the north . . . he stood still, with a strange bewilderment in his eyes, as if transfixed by some kind of tremendous shock. Then he swayed on his legs; and sank in a lifeless heap by the drifted bank of the pool."

A sentimental writer, this man who never smiled. In New York he shared an apartment with his cousin Bliss Carman who went about in a wide-brimmed felt hat with a "fresh blonde face and wild mop of hair." Big melancholic Bliss with his half-baked ideas about Personal Harmonizing and his over-baked poetry, long out of fashion, almost an embarrassment. Except that I don't find him embarrassing at all.

Just interesting. Everything seems much more interesting than it once did.

• • •

Why, Salman Rushdie wants to know, would Dorothy want to go home when home is Kansas?

It seems to me that he both gets the point and misses it. Loving something which isn't entirely likeable — a place that no one takes seriously or a person riddled with faults — is a good love, and a hard love to come by. If Kansas were as appealing as Emerald City, Dorothy's homesickness wouldn't be nearly so poignant and the story wouldn't have the same emotional pull: the tension of choosing something which is clearly less and yet somehow more. Dorothy's fondness for Glinda is one thing; her love for Aunt Em, and Aunt Em's love for her are something else again.

But when I discuss the article with friends they agree with Rushdie. Kansas would have killed Dorothy, they say. There is no such thing as "home." Why do I think I'll be happier in Canada? Why bother? It makes no sense to anyone here, but then my explanations are never very good.

Even if they were it wouldn't matter. Home, when home is Canada, doesn't convince anyone.

I try to imagine Dorothy not going home. If she made the journey only to discover that the place she came to was better than the place she left, then I suppose you would have the typical American tale: arriving at the pot of gold. And I suppose in its very retreat from Emerald City and its return to black and white Kansas, in its insistence on a return to beginnings, the story is un-American.

And yet Rushdie is right too. What would happen if Dorothy stayed in Kansas for ever?

"Are we to think," asks Rushdie, "that Dorothy has learned no more on her journey than that she didn't need to make such a journey in the first place?"

Well, no. She made the journey in order to see that what was beyond the rainbow was under her nose. It takes a long time, and usually a journey, to see with fresh eyes what we've looked at for so long. The desire to return to our beginnings is an old animal instinct. We aren't in touch with it much anymore, with any instinct; and so it confuses more than it clarifies because it is so simple, and everything else is not. Animals return to spawn and die, or to spawn and leave. The pattern is one of returning to leave, rather than returning to stay.

I remember my typically Canadian response to the invitation to meet other Canadians. Was it at the consulate? Was it organized by the University of Toronto? I didn't go. Canadians don't drift towards each other. We may be proud to be Canadian, but embarrassed to be one of many, convinced we would have nothing in common except an embarrassing straightness we don't want underscored.

You can be homesick and shy at the same time. You can love Canada without thinking that living Canadians, encountered randomly, have anything to do with that love. You can enjoy reading about Canadians in a cool and large library without wanting to meet them in the flesh. Gould loved the Arctic even though he never got farther north than Churchill. The love was real. It was a love of the imagination, and that's probably what Canada is for me.

That's the point that Rushdie misses. Kansas becomes a part of Dorothy's imagined world. The place we come from becomes a part of our imagined reality, every bit as much as Oz.

A Poland Springs truck goes by, dark green with its name in white letters on the side. Glenn Gould always drank Poland Springs water. He used to go into a restaurant and order it, then listen to all the conversations around him, better able to hear one thing if he heard other things at the same time.

Whenever he had trouble playing a passage of music, he set up radios next to the piano and turned them up loud — drowning out the sound of self-doubt. He was more in touch with the music, less distracted by himself, when slightly removed. He handled self-doubt the way he handled cold, by adding layer upon layer of sound.

And now it starts to rain. I turn on a lamp. The rain (the lamp) makes me much more visible than before.

Hard rain thumps against the windows, and the long empty apartment seems full of animals. My heart beats faster. Little feet on the floor.

In the fairy tale I was reading yesterday, a spell entered a boy's finger and turned him into a dog, then a thief slashed his paw and he returned to human form. But what if you don't want to return to what you were?

Is there a way of breaking the spell so that the captive comes home but as something more than she was?

Fred and Ginger

It is mild, mid-December, my daughter's birthday. I tell her that she was born in Canada and some day we'll move back. Halifax, I've been thinking lately: the coastline, the history, the pretty valleys beyond.

"Do you know anyone in Halifax?" asks Alec.

"No."

Sochi and I watch *The Gay Divorcee* for the third time and then we all head out to buy a Christmas tree. We've been inside all day and I'm looking forward to going from forest to forest along Broadway, but Alec stops at the first one. He asks the price of the tree, and it becomes clear that we have differences on this score too. He wants a big tree, I want a small one. We stand next to the evergreens, a hundred of them propped against a long wooden stand, and argue.

The Gay Divorcee has the most explicitly sexual dance I've seen Fred and Ginger do. It comes at the end of Fred's long chase and Ginger's headstrong flight. Fred sings Cole Porter's "Night and Day" — wanting to spend the rest of his life "making love to you" — and when they dance it's pursuit — resistance — coupling, pursuit — resistance — coupling, as Ginger pushes him away, her hand on his chin, and he spins back off balance, then follows her one last time to a climax and lowers her onto a soft pillow-like bench. He offers her a cigarette. She looks up at him amazed, and he looks down at her, entirely pleased with himself.

The music goes through my head as we squabble in front of two vendors and both children. Alec is saying we'll make room by moving things out of the way, and I'm saying there's no place to move things to. The squabble has its effect: the vendors lower the price and we get a beautiful tree.

They truss it up by pulling it through a drum which wraps it with plastic netting. We ask where the trees come from. "Canada," the vendor says. "Where in Canada?" She smiles and shrugs. "I don't know where in Canada. It's a place called Atlanta but I don't know where it is."

Alec shoulders the tree and looks at the tag on the trunk. Nova Scotia. The trees are from the Atlantic provinces.

"You see, it's in the cards," I say to Alec. "We're moving to Halifax."

"You think so."

"Well then, Quebec. Let's move to Quebec."

A few weeks ago a woman from Montreal told me that I should move there but as an American. "Quebeckers don't like Canadians," she said, "but they like Americans."

We decorate the tree with little Mexican ornaments made of straw and paper. "This must remind you of your childhood," says Alec. "No," I say, "it makes me think of Mexico." I rethread many of them, little paper and cotton-batten birds, the worse for wear, and hang them on Nova Scotia.

Last night I read Donald Creighton's account of the fall of Quebec. "Montcalm made a last effort. He ordered La Guienne up to the heights at once. And, to his face, Vaudreuil countermanded the order. Tomorrow he would see about the defences of Anse au Foulon. Tomorrow: tomorrow was September 13th."

Montcalm and Wolfe met on the Plains of Abraham on September 13th, 1759. Wolfe, tall and gawky. Montcalm, in his green uniform open at the front. Both men died that day — Wolfe in victory, Montcalm in defeat. The year 1759 marked the end of New France; it paved the way for my family's presence two hundred years later as we listened to the Queen before we opened our gifts on Christmas day. Always the Queen — her radio address at ten in the morning — and usually the prime minister too, though my father was less strict about that. The enforced wait amused my parents and made me choke.

I realize as I read Creighton's history of Canada that my impulse to move to Halifax is almost an historical one. New York was the last great port in British hands. Thousands of loyalists "overflowed the accommodation of the city and filled the camps which were established on Long Island, Staten Island, and the adjacent shores of New Jersey. In those last hectic days of preparation and departure that followed the peace, it seemed that 'everybody, all the world, moves on to Nova Scotia.'" During the spring and summer of 1783, great fleets sailed from New York carrying nearly thirty thousand loyalists to their new homes in the north.

Seven inches of snow have fallen. Sochi and Ben wade into snowdrifts and make angels in the postage stamp spaces in front of highrises. The sky is dark, the city black and white. I have that old forsaken feeling you get when you come home after being away, or remain behind when someone leaves.

Something beginning? Or something ending? The snow is so familiar and yet, in the context, so distinctive: the snow less than it is, New York more than it is. Perfect for snowballs, lousy for angels. A slight rain is falling, a film-like crust has already formed.

We go to the park and slide down the hill. The sycamores are here, covered with snow, and in elegant rows as they are in Paris.

This is the thought that steadies me. The sycamores look like Paris. It's so much easier to be somewhere when it reminds you of somewhere else.

If I were in Canada, I would need that slide into somewhere else just as children need to be someone else. My mother put herself to sleep in Renfrew by designing couturier dresses. This place is not quite this place. And I'm not quite me.

What is it that motivates such imaginings? I suppose it's hope.

• • •

My mother gathers the soft underhair of musk-oxen off low arctic willows, and brings it home. She spreads a newspaper on her lap and shakes bits of dirt out of the hair, combing it with her fingers, separating the strands. A small pile of arctic debris rises up on the paper: sand, dirt, very fine bits of moss, willow leaves, twigs.

She tells me that the area around Eureka is called the Garden of the Arctic. On the other side of Eureka's Black Hills runs Hot Weather Creek — an area full of musk-oxen because of the denser vegetation: arctic willows and various mosses are abundant.

There may be something pathetic about clinging to this border, a border which makes no sense when you talk about native peoples, or even Quebec, but it's all we have — a line marking us off as a northern people.

The Eighth Remove

It's my country, my native land, and I love it. You don't love because: you love despite; not for the virtues, but despite the faults.

WILLIAM FAULKNER

Going Home

Snow, like jello, has set. Yesterday morning's snowfall immediately turned to slush, but in the afternoon the temperature dropped, and at night the air was crisp. The new snow is dry.

The radio reports another murder for a coat: a sixteen-year-old boy was wearing a leather jacket with an eightball on the back, he refused to give it up, and two others shot him. Lately, when people ask for money, they preface it by complimenting you on your coat. "Nice coat," they say. And then, "Can you spare some change?"

Sochi and I walk down Broadway. "There's always garbage, isn't there," I say.

"Yes," she says, "that's why we're moving to Canada. They don't throw garbage in the snow."

The flakes are thicker and softer now. I imagine the ground between here and Canada going white.

I call information for Michael Snow's number, and phone him. I say that I'm coming to Toronto for five days and ask if I can talk to him. I say, "I'd like to know how your time in New York fits in with the rest of your life."

"It doesn't," he answers. "It doesn't matter anymore." And he repeats, "It doesn't. That's the simple answer."

But he agrees to see me. He tells me to come to the place where he plays piano and trumpet on Monday nights.

I call Joyce Wieland and am surprised by the little girl quality of her voice, a Billie Holiday voice. "I'm coming home," I say, "to find the end to the book I'm writing."

New York disappears almost immediately into cloud. It's brighter up here, in the cloud, and now in the blue. Breakfast arrives; the pats of butter are shaped like flowers (in Mexico

Margaret Trudeau ate butter shaped like roses). The three people behind me are all Canadians. The loud and talkative one asks for tea, then tells the others about walking down Fifth Avenue behind a family all dressed up for the Easter parade. The woman was wearing too much makeup and a Sears Roebuck dress, "but trying," the father was busy unwrapping two lollipops and dropping the wrappers on the sidewalk. "I picked up the wrappers, knelt down and said to the two little girls, 'Tell your Daddy he should throw his trash in the garbage can.'"

The dark-skinned man beside me doesn't take off his duffel coat despite the warmth. He gives me his creamers when coffee arrives, and we share a pen to fill out the customs forms. When the plane starts its descent he says, "Some kind of weather."

The ground below is flat and snowy; fields are marked off by thin lines of trees — a body, most of its hair plucked out. Low buildings come into view, then black and white airport markers, then yellow grass sticking up through snow. We wait for a long time before the plane pulls up to the terminal. Mr. Loud and Talkative says that Toronto airport has been rated for efficiency, and it's in the bottom ten.

I take the bus into town and get off into deep snow — surprising for Toronto — and cold. I wait for a streetcar on Queen Street. I have Joyce Wieland's address in my pocket.

She welcomes me by saying, "You've come back to the thirties depression." A large woman with tiny fingers discoloured by years of paint. Her face is soft and wide, and her earlobes are very large.

She takes me through her chilly house with its warm colours: blue, mustard, light pink, terra cotta around the fireplace. A stuffed goose stands in the middle of a long table, a stuffed beaver occupies a bench. She bought the beaver for forty-five dollars from Britnell's antique store when she first got back, "a rabid nationalist," from New York. She takes me into the kitchen and makes tea, all the while talking anxiously about present financial worries and ones that loom ahead; and furiously about Mulroney.

I listen, aware that something is wrong. Underneath her friendliness and anxiety something is shifting, the ground is giving way. Events seem to have collapsed together in her mind. The move into the house, her return from New York, her separation from Michael Snow — they all seem to have happened in the same year. She tells me that she was on the phone last night to Greg Curnoe telling him that this was the end. He reassured her. He is wonderful at reminding her, she says, of other things. "But then his family came in for dinner, we were only able to talk a few minutes. I hope we can talk longer tonight." Wistful, desperate.

After her parents died, her sister used to sit beside her at bedtime and tell her the story of Joan of Arc burning at the stake. The image of flames around a woman appears in her violent and angry paintings of the eighties. She says it was all the hate and rage and depression that made her brain go. It happens to a lot of women, she says. We talk about her breakup with Snow. She says that a friend told her that what goes around comes around, "but I don't see him suffering."

Upstairs in her tidy studio, there's a photograph of her in her twenties. She is sitting on the floor, her back against the wall, her hair bleached, her face serious, lush, sad. Snow's trumpet hangs from a nail above her head. We look at the photograph and she says, "There's the trumpet."

Small back yards extend to King Street and the streetcars going by. The snow on the sidewalks is fresh and deep, and even on the street it's still a blonde-brown. This part of Toronto has brick houses, smallscale streets with a network of wires for the streetcars, and light snow still falling.

The subway could be a train station in the country: clean, low-ceilinged, new, well-lit. I sit down in the train and the seat gives way — cushioned vinyl — how quickly a knife would penetrate. On the wall above the seat, a transit sign says, *Our Riders Write*: " . . . the feet on seats problem is better. But you still have those people who believe that they can stretch out their legs and block the aisle." Ms V.H. Toronto.

How benign everything seems. I feel as though I've taken a helmet off my head.

On my friend Sheila's street, the snowbanks are high and white, the houses modest in size, the street snow-packed (a heavy snowfall the night before I arrived, and enough cold to keep it).

When Sheila was a child, her father would take her and her brothers and sister to cemeteries and tell them stories about the people buried there. He would drive out to old invisible historic sites, and leave them in the car while he questioned farmers working in the fields. She grew up knowing that Canada can hold someone's interest for a lifetime. And now she is telling me — this friend I've known for twelve years — that the country isn't going to make it, "and it's our fault. If we don't care enough about it, if we only care about getting from A to B with the least trouble, if snow is the enemy and being cold is inferior, if we can't even identify with this aspect of Canada . . ."

She has quizzed her young students. How many of you have been to Saskatchewan? No one put up a hand. How many of you have been to Disneyland? Everyone put up a hand. How many of you have heard of Saskatchewan? One child put up her hand.

"There's something about our history," says Sheila, "which leaves no impression. Immigrants don't learn that we have a body of history and therefore a body of obligations. They come here and are told they'll have the freedom to keep all their traditions alive, and so they create a nicer version of Romania, or Germany, or Hungary, and don't ever feel a larger allegiance."

From the basement she brings up old issues of *The Beaver* magazine for me to look at. I scan her ceiling-high shelves of books about the north, her father's painstaking card catalogue of all his books and files, his story in *The Beaver* about finding the remains of Fort Qu'Appelle, and I'm filled with the quiet knowledge — the quiet joy — that this is the history I want to know. I'm reminded of Emily Carr searching for totem poles before they completely disappeared.

Joyce Wieland's kitchen was full of large white poinsettias, small red poinsettias, a towering pink amaryllis, and light. When I asked about the marriage she withdrew — or was I tired — or did the two coincide? Her withdrawal, so that our conversation faltered as I got ready to leave.

Her marriage broken up, her country breaking up, her mind. I asked her what happened to her nationalism and she said it was still here. "I still feel I would get out there and fight. But the country is tired and confused. You never know what the fuck Mulroney's going to do. He makes everybody drunk, in a way, or powerless. He's here to dismantle Canada, and he's done it. There's very little left." She used two words to describe the state of the country: numbness and fear. "It's never happened to us that we have such a thing — that maybe it'll just not be there."

"What will be there instead?"

"The same numbness the Americans feel. I remember being there — it's like a death."

Surprised to be so cold. Surprised at how cold cold is. I touched Wieland's beaver and the fur felt dusty, dry, wiry, dead.

I take the streetcar on King over to University, walk up to Dundas Street, and over to the Art Gallery of Ontario. The Canadian section is upstairs: two rooms, one with a smattering of work by various people — early Borduas, early Lawren Harris — the other room devoted to the Group of Seven. I look for more but there isn't any more.

Downstairs, at the desk, a pleasant young man with a

ponytail says, "Don't panic." He explains that two of the galleries are under renovation, and opens a catalogue to show me a picture of a Michael Snow construction I might have seen: the final shot of waves in his film *Wavelength* has been reproduced thirty times and assembled in a grid as a way of fixing "something which has stopped within the flux of what's going on."

Years ago I watched my parents spread white gauze curtains over the old black cherry tree in the back. The wind caught the soft gauze, and then my mother caught it and pinned it down.

"Last year," she said, "the birds got every last one."

It was a perfect summer day, warm and light and clear. My parents moved through the garden as though caught in some other world of newborn air: my father kneeling on freshly cut grass, my mother trailing gauze. The sort of day we can't believe, knowing how transitory summer is, yet do believe, aware of all the summers past, of things that don't last but do continue.

"What was that quotation?" I asked her. "The one you got so excited about a few years ago."

"Yes," and she bent her head to remember.

"Every breath you take contains three atoms of nitrogen breathed by ancient man, and five by Tyrannosaurus Rex."

Scents, dangers, fears, food, progeny, desire. Sweet William grew under the cherry tree. And something my father called yellow primroses, although he said that wasn't the proper name.

Upstairs, I walk through the rooms more slowly and stop in front of a painting by Pegi Nicol MacLeod. The label says, Born in Listowel, 1904, died in New York, 1949.

Pegi Nicol MacLeod called her paintings peculiar, overcrowded things. She herself was peculiar and over- crowded: a short woman with a "pug nose, big mouth, brights lipstick" who talked constantly. She moved to New York after marrying Norman MacLeod. In 1940, after three years in Manhattan, she went "homesick and broke" to Fredericton, New Brunswick to teach art. It became her second home: she spent summers in Fredericton and winters in New York. In 1945, she wrote to a Canadian friend: "I really loathe New York. The beautiful parts don't enter my everyday life." In 1947, her *Manhattan Cycle* began a tour of Canada — forty-two paintings which she called alternatively *Canadian Painter in New York* or *Black Life from a Fifth Floor Window*.

Her personal life was a dark version of her ebullient, overabundant paintings: an overcrowded combination of homesickness and heartsickness. "I rarely see him," she said of Norman; he had a lover; she herself was dying. In the last two months of her life, she said in a letter that she was "painting madly" and had conceived a "whole new view of colour." One of her last paintings was *Ripe World*, a complex mixture of women, children, and jungle growth with large areas of orange. It was described by one critic as both abstract and jazzy, and full of a kind of terrible grief. She died of cancer at the age of forty-five and was buried in Fredericton. She's known there, almost revered, and little known elsewhere in the country.

The reference library is full, it's Sunday afternoon. A glass elevator takes you up to the fourth floor. This is where I used to sit and read Champlain's narratives before I went to Mexico. I look out the window, and down below the red and black Donut World globe turns just as it did eight years ago. Across the street there's a parking lot, a range of skyscrapers to the left, a wooded area to the right which must be Rosedale.

Harold Town had the most magnificent magnolia in Rosedale. He died just before Christmas, still famous if no longer so much admired, a prolific painter who refused to go to New York, refused to let the New York critic Clement Greenberg even look at his work, even refused to use American paints. Joyce Wieland mentioned Town — the lingering cancer at the end of which nothing was left.

The last thing she said, as I laced up my boots and she sat on the stairs, was that when we die we make a journey to the centre and are renewed. She and her nephew, she said, have made some journeys "through the wormholes."

In 1978, she was sitting beside a window in the print shop in Cape Dorset and "began to notice light more . . . certain kinds of radiances around the edges of objects. And I began to see the primary colours, the breakdown, which I had never noticed before . . ."

It's four in the afternoon. The sky has turned grey. I realize that my only relationship with New York is leaving, and my only relationship with Canada is coming back.

I continue to collect stories, finding out more about Mack Sennett, the king of comic silent pictures who lapsed after talk, and Marie Prevost, the bathing beauty whose dog ate her after she died — building a mythology of the inarticulate: "dumb" animals, Eskimos in New York, silent movie stars who couldn't make the transition to talk; people born in Canada, coming to New York, petering out elsewhere. A folklore of self-deprecation and self-doubt. (The art critic Lucy Lippard said that Wieland "found her tongue in another kind of silence, a gentle but fragmented and disjunctive serialism with a narrative line above or below the surface.")

Dame Emma Albani, born Marie-Louise-Cécile-Emma Lajeunesse in Chambly, Quebec in 1847, sang at the Met in New York from 1891 to 1892. Her remarkable voice is preserved on a Rococo 5255 recording on which she sings eight titles including turn-of-the-century songs and three Handel arias.

Eva Tanguay, born in 1878 in Marbleton, Quebec, became the "I Don't Care Girl." She first sang "I Don't Care" on Broadway in 1904, earned $3,500 a week, and for a while was the richest actress in Vaudeville. Famous for madcap humour, freakish costumes, a frizzy mop of hair and buck teeth, she performed Salome in 1908, dressed, she said, in "two pearls."

> *I don't care, I don't care*
> *If I do get the mean and stony stare,*
> *If I'm never successful, it won't be distressful*
> *'Cos I don't care.*

She lost her fortune in 1929, and in 1933 went blind. Sophie Tucker paid for the operations that restored her sight. She died in 1947, crippled by arthritis and without a penny.

I look up Michael Snow. Born in Toronto in 1929, he represented Canada at the Venice Biennale in 1970, had a retrospective at the Art Gallery of Ontario the same year, and a major exhibition in 1979 which toured Lucerne, Bonn and Munich; his experimental films have received critical acclaim in the United States and Europe.

He is funnier, shorter, and snowier than I expected. His eyebrows and eyelashes are very white and, contrary to photographs in which he never smiles, he laughs a lot. On Monday nights he plays at the Music Gallery near Joyce Wieland's childhood library at Dovercourt and Queen. (She remembers reaching for a book on low shelves and pulling out Beatrix Potter. "It fixed me," she said. The delicate, intimate, small-scale version of life.) A second man plays guitar and synthesizer, a third invents vocal noises — words, bleats, snatches of poetry. Usually one or two other musicians show up, but not tonight. Snow wears black pants, brown thick-soled shoes, a checked shirt.

They play, themes come up and they stick with them or not, but they don't think anything out ahead. The group goes by the name CCMC: Canadian Collective Music Company. Snow tries to sell me two tapes for fifteen dollars, and I tell him I'm poor.

A young man arrives and congratulates him on the

recording they did together. Snow is pleased. In an aside, he tells me that it was kind of charming to be asked to play by these young musicians, and refers to himself as "an old duffer." But when he hears the recording and finds the young man's piano far louder than his trumpet, he doesn't hesitate to say — jokingly but unmistakeably — that the piano is too loud. Nor when he yells up goodnight to the young man in the studio, and gets no answer, does he hesitate to say, "Fuck you too."

Two images stay with me: Snow with his young wife, young friends, young admirers — vigorous, prosperous, and full of edgy self-respect. And Wieland with her cat, her stuffed beaver, her stuffed goose — at an early end of her rope.

Canada always manages a stable precariousness, nothing showy, which is painful and on some level endearing. A friend tells me that this time Quebec will separate, but this time means "in her lifetime."

In New York I put my whole soul into being Canadian, which reduced and confused me even while it steadied me — what is it after all? But without it would I be anything?

Here, it's simple. I'm home. Home is somewhere knowable, that you want to know.

At the library I watch a video made of Gould's last recording of *The Goldberg Variations*. The director describes the variations using Gould's words — thirty remarkable views of an unremarkable ground base theme — and then the camera moves to the forty-nine-year-old pianist: glasses pushed back on his forehead, feet up on the console. He leans back in an orange chair and smiles as he talks, then conducts himself as he listens back to himself on tape. The camera moves in a long slow sweep from inside the control room through the glass window to Gould behind the piano: balding, overweight, shoulders hunched, dressed in black, a prematurely old man who plays more exquisitely than ever, and who will be dead within the year.

After his father died, Alec called his mother and got his father's voice; the message on the answering machine hadn't been erased. Here is Gould's ghost. His voice, face, fingers. (His humming was louder on recordings made in Toronto because the air was dryer than in New York.)

Across the street, at Lichtman's, I pick up a copy of George Grant's *Lament for a Nation*. Grant saw Canada's future as early as the forties: a branch plant economy dependent on American capital and subservient to American thinking, always dependent, and bound to disappear. The name continues, like the maiden name of a woman whose children consume her life.

Joyce Wieland quilted I LOVE CANADA. She didn't care what people thought. She poured out her love of country, the love inspired by her stay in New York, and its expression made possible by the city's arrogance, armour, innocence.

After she returned to Canada, her work became overtly nationalistic and environmental: beautiful water quilts, delicate flowers, written messages. And then, after the breakup with Snow, violent, dream-like, mythological. Beginning again.

In the beginning, trappers travelled across Canada with beaver castor tied in pouches to their waists. They set out in canoes and roamed a wilderness necessary for their own survival, a glittering network of rivers and lakes, an interconnected waterway: without wilderness, no furs. The United States quickly became a country of farms and towns, while Canada remained a country of travellers.

In the small dining room lined with Sheila's books, stories are everywhere, in the soft carpet and textured wallpaper, in the chairs still warm from other people and the books still warm from Sheila's hands. I see her face, kind, intelligent, disappointed, and soft, wearing the disappointment Canadians feel in themselves. And yet here we are, at the source of all the stories we could ever want to know.

• • •

It's wet and grey. Take-off is delayed because one passenger has been rejected by American immigration. His bag, already on board, has to be taken off. What other country would allow American immigration to operate on its soil?

Smell of airplane coffee. Slight trace of snow on the grassy far reaches of the airport. We rise up through soft cloud which moves like a transparent scarf over the city, and I fly into New York with a gin and tonic and three packages of peanuts in my stomach, *Lament for a Nation* in my lap. The book ends with a quote from the *Aeneid*. "They were holding their arms outstretched in love toward the further shore."

Underfoot, the sidewalk is crusty and wet from melting snow. I step out of the cab with my golden suitcase, cinnamon-coloured said Joyce Wieland, a little bag of spices. Marco Polo stayed away for twenty-six years and had to slit open his tattered coat and let jewels pour out before anyone believed him.

I've been away only five days and my gifts are a few ribbons and mugs. And so at the top of the front steps I grab Alec by the collar and, laughing, shove him against the front door.

"When?" I ask him. "We're moving to Canada and I want to know when."

"All right," and he is laughing too.

From New Jersey comes the smell of roasting coffee. Winds carry it across the Hudson and through Riverside Park to our doorstep. Behind us the little tree is bathed in sunlight.

In my happiness I get my hair cut short, and I buy lipstick. Sober widow turns into gay divorcee now that she's leaving New York.

Acknowledgements and Sources

Thanks to the editors of *This Magazine* and *The Malahat Review* who published portions of the work in progress.

Thanks to Belinda Kaye at the American Museum of Natural History in New York City for her generous archival assistance.

My special thanks to Stan Dragland, Bob Sherrin, Tom Riordan, and, as always, Mark Fried on whom I relied for editorial advice and encouragement; and to the following authors whose books informed and inspired this one: Kenn Harper, *Give Me My Father's Body: The Life of Minik, the New York Eskimo* (Iqaluit: Blacklead Books, 1986); Howard Norman, *Where the Chill Came From* (San Francisco: North Point Press, 1982) and *The Wishing Bone Cycle* (Santa Barbara: Ross-Erickson Publishing, 1982); Paula Blanchard, *The Life of Emily Carr* (Vancouver: Douglas & McIntyre, 1987); The Art Gallery of Ontario's catalogue, *Joyce Wieland*, with its articles by Marie Fleming and Lucy Lippard (Toronto: Key Porter Books, 1987); Otto Friedrich, *Glenn Gould: A Life and Variations* (Toronto: Lester & Orpen Dennys, 1989); Geoffrey Payzant, *Glenn Gould, Music & Mind* (Toronto: Van Nostrand Reinhold, 1978); Philip Marchand, *Marshall McLuhan: The Medium and the Messenger* (Toronto: Random House of Canada, 1989); James Polk, *Wilderness Writers* (Toronto: Clarke, Irwin, 1972); Harry Rasky, *Stratas: An Affectionate Tribute* (Toronto: Oxford University Press, 1988); Dennis Reid, *A Concise History of Canadian Painting* (Toronto: Oxford University Press, 1988); Farley Mowat's trilogy *Tundra, The Polar Passion, Ordeal by Ice* (Toronto: McClelland and Stewart, 1973); Joan Murray, *Daffodils in Winter: The Life and Letters of Pegi Nicol MacLeod* (Moonbeam, Ont.: Penumbra Press, 1984); George Whalley, *The Legend of John Hornby* (Toronto: Macmillan of Canada, 1977).